The Story of Art

From the British Museum, reproduced in Egyptian Tomb Paintings, by courtesy of Faber and Faber, Ltd.

Guests and Musicians, from a Chapel of the 18th Dynasty

The Pantheon Story of Art
for Young People

A REVISED UP-TO-DATE EDITION

Ariane Ruskin Batterberry

PANTHEON BOOKS

ACKNOWLEDGMENTS

I would like to acknowledge the great kindness of the National Gallery of
Art, Washington, D.C., in permitting me the use of some fifty-one color plates,
as well as many black-and-white photographs, in the production of this book.
I would also like to thank Mr. Hellmut Wohl for his introduction and excellent editorial advice, Mr. Carter Brown of the National Gallery of Art for
his assistance in the choice of illustrations, and Mr. Mark Roskill, of the Fogg
Museum, Harvard University, for his expert aid in writing two chapters. The
Greek Press and Information Service have generously supplied me with a large
number of photographs of works of art that are to be found in Greece.

Ariane Ruskin Batterberry

The publisher would like to thank
The Copifyer Lithograph Corporation
for its special efforts to achieve true color reproduction
of the works of art represented in this book

Frontis: Saint Eustace, by Dürer
from the National Gallery of Art, Washington, D.C.
Gallatin Collection

Foto-Ent-Roma. Istituto Italiano di Cultura

Copyright © 1964, 1975 by Ariane Ruskin Batterberry
All rights reserved under International and Pan-American Copyright Conventions.
Published in the United States by Pantheon Books, a division of
Random House, Inc., and simultaneously in Canada by Random House of Canada
Limited, Toronto. Manufactured in the United States of America.
Library of Congress Cataloging in Publication Data
Batterberry, Ariane Ruskin. The Pantheon story of art for young people.
Summary: Surveys the history of art in the western world from prehistoric cave
paintings to modern abstracts emphasizing the major works and artists of each
period. Includes a brief discussion of the art of Asia, Africa, and the South Seas.
1. Art—History—Juvenile literature. [1. Art—History] I. Title. II. Title: Story of art.
N5302.B28   1975   709   74-24717   ISBN 0-394-83107-1
2 4 6 8 0 9 7 5 3 1

DESIGNED BY PATRICIA DE GROOT

Introduction

We live in an age when adults spend more time devising ingenious ways to instruct, stimulate, and entertain children than ever before. The particular delight of this volume which Miss Ruskin has written for children on the history of art is that it does so with a rarely found grace, simplicity, and charm. Since the time of the Romantics we have come to believe in the great potentiality of children's intuitive perceptions, more spontaneous and vital than our rational, complex, and detached modes of experiencing things. Miss Ruskin does so; but beyond this she also understands, in a way that few of us possess so articulately and finely, the intellectual capacities of children.

In writing a history of art for adults, an author may feel that he must interest his reader sufficiently to convince him that art is worth spending his time on. One of Miss Ruskin's qualities is that she knows that her readers do not demand this. Children are in and out of themselves interested in and alive to art. If they are not always, as the Romantics at times imagined, artists, at least they do, almost all of them, make art—by drawing, painting, or modeling. They experience the works of others vividly; and they take art seriously. Knowing this, and respecting children's natural abilities to see and judge, Miss Ruskin has given them the directions they need in order to bring into play and unfold these qualities. She has told them what kind of people made the art of the past, why it was made, and about the beliefs, legends, and events that are represented in art. She has supplied information and explanation so that the history of art may become part of children's imaginative world. And she has familiarized them with the changing modes in the language of art, of form and style.

Miss Ruskin deals, as she must in writing for children, with essentials. Her lively manner of doing so is based on sound, scholarly art-historical knowledge and insight. Children are indeed to be envied for having such a pleasurable book.

Hellmut Wohl, Yale University

*Saint-Martin
and the Beggar
by El Greco*

Contents

to my Father

The Story of Art

Drawing of the Head of a Woman by Leonardo da Vinci

Reindeer, from Font-de-Gaume in France

I

Cave Painting

Who painted the first painting? When did art begin? We do not know. But we do know that man has been an artist for a very long time. In fact, we have remains of his art that are even older than the traces of his first houses or earliest pottery.

How did art begin? Perhaps early man noticed that some accidental lines he had scribbled, or the claw mark of an animal on the ground, resembled some creature he often saw, and tried to repeat the image or make it more like the model. Or perhaps he wanted to keep count of how many animals he had killed, and tried to record it by some scratches on a stone which looked like one of the animals themselves. We can never know exactly how it came about, but men were very early skilled at copying the things they saw by the use of lines.

We find the first paintings, along with the very first traces of man as we know him today, in the caves in which he lived during the Stone Age. This was the time when the last glaciers of the Ice Age advanced and retreated over the globe. England and Scandinavia and the mountain ranges of the rest of Europe were covered with snow and ice. Men lived huddled around fires in the warmest and most protected places they could find—caves. They did not grow food but hunted wild animals that provided the meat they ate and the skins they used for clothing. They used animal bones and stone for such tools as they had, and their lives were hard and brutal, yet they painted some of the loveliest pictures in the history of art.

The cave paintings we have were found only during the past hundred years, mostly in Spain and France. Some were discovered by exploration and some quite by chance. For example, a group of boys, looking for a lost dog, dug a hole in the ground and fell into the cave of Lascaux, the most beautifully painted in France.

These caves served as dwellings from about 60,000 B.C. to 10,000 B.C., ten times the period which separates us from the first Pharaohs and pyramids of Egypt! And yet, the lives of the cave men and even their paintings changed very little, for man's start was a slow and painful one.

As the climate of Europe was much colder than it is now, the cave men painted animals that are now found much farther north—bears and reindeer, as well as some that have since died out altogether, such as the woolly rhinoceros, the great shaggy elephant-like mammoth, and even an animal resembling the unicorn. We see, too, pictures of bison that now live only in North America, and two kinds of horses, a small type like a Shetland pony and a larger type like the modern horse. Once in a while there are little stick figures representing the men themselves, sometimes disguised in animal skins for some magic ritual, but most often in hunting scenes, such as the picture of a stag hunt from Castellón in Spain.

Were the pictures colored? They certainly were!

In fact, the paints are so bright today that they cannot have faded much in the past 50,000 years! The early artist used natural colors from the soil— red and yellow, along with lampblack from the lamps with which he lit his cave. There are some traces of blue and green, but these colors were difficult to make and rarely used, as animals and men were always the subject and a background that might have trees and other vegetation was never painted.

Sometimes the outline of a picture was etched into a stone, and sometimes a whole animal was painted on a bump in the rock, or actually carved or sculpted in clay, so that it would appear to stand out from the wall, floor, or ceiling of the cave.

From Art of the Stone Age, ©*Holle and Co. Verlag, Baden-Baden, Germany, 1961*

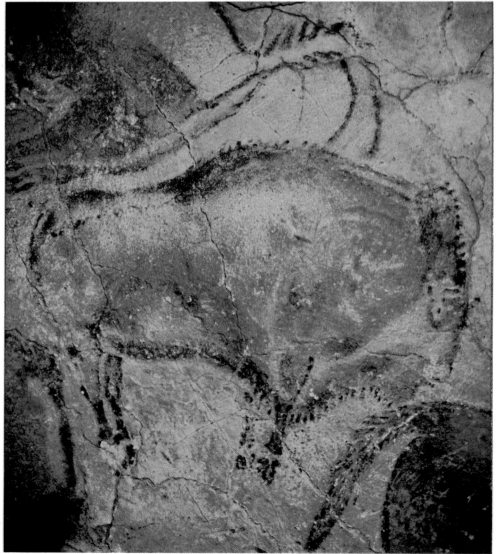

*Standing Bison,
from Altamira in Spain*

Bison Sculptured in Clay, from Tuc d'Audoubert in France

From Art of the Stone Age, ©Holle and Co. Verlag, Baden-Baden, Germany, 1961

The artists' tools were surprisingly like those of today. A tube of bone containing red paint powder, a neatly sharpened crayon made of colored earth, and a piece of bone that had served as a palette have been found. Feathers or animal hairs may well have been used as brushes, and the soft, furry coats of animals may sometimes have been depicted by spraying on powdered color with blowguns made of hollow bones. Strangest of all, ancient artists, like modern ones, seem to have made sketches—on small stones.

Of course, over such a long period of time, the method of the cave painters changed and improved. At first, they may have merely made flat outline drawings, and only later have found ways of making their figures rounded, with shadows and an appearance of modeling. Still, even from the very beginning, the drawings were lively and realistic. Animals were shown in every position— resting, standing, running, or shot with arrows and dying—and the artist had no trouble in making his meaning clear. See, for example, the picture of a galloping boar from Altamira in Spain. Have you ever seen an animal more perfectly caught in the act of jumping?

We have already decided that we do not know how or when painting began. Why, then, did man paint at all? This is just as much a mystery. Men may have painted for the pure pleasure of representing what they saw and enjoying the decoration of colorful pictures in their dwellings. Or it may be that they wanted to keep a record of past events,

Stag Hunt, from Castellón in Spain

Courtesy of the American Museum of Natural History

5

Wild Boar, from Altamira in Spain

such as an unusually successful hunt. In the stag hunt we have seen, almost every animal seems to have been hit. But the paintings are often in small dark areas or eerie narrow passages where it would have been difficult to see them. Why should this be? Were they part of a magic spell? Ancient man may have felt, as many primitive tribes do today,

that he might more easily kill an animal in the hunt if he painted a picture of it beforehand.

The skill of the cave painter died out long before history began, and the secrets of art have been relearned many times since. This is the story we are going to trace.

II
The Pyramid Builders

Many thousands of years passed between the days of the cave men and those of the Pharaohs, the kings of Egypt who built the great Pyramids, and during this time men learned to grow food on the land and to join together to form tribes and nations. It is with the Egyptians, though, before any other people, that the story of art really begins, for the art of the cave men was already long buried and forgotten, but the work of the Egyptians remained for many centuries as a model for later artists.

The valley of the Nile, in which the Egyptians lived, was very fertile because rich soil was carried down from the highlands of Abyssinia to the south and deposited on the plain by the rising of the river every year, and they were protected from the attacks of other peoples because their land was surrounded by an uncrossable desert. Their history begins around 3000 B.C., or about five thousand years ago, when King Menes united the many small kingdoms in the Nile valley into one great realm under his rule. He was the founder of what is called the first "dynasty," or family of rulers,

and there were thirty-one such "dynasties" or families in the history of Egypt. The kings after Menes were called "Pharaohs" and they were considered gods by their people, who obeyed their every wish.

The Egyptians had a strange belief, and this is why so much of their art work remains for us today. They thought that a man's soul would continue to live after death if his body were preserved and statues of him were made and kept. For this reason, their Pharaohs had huge tombs constructed, among them the great Pyramids we know, built for the kings Cheops, Chephren, and Mycerinus. These great stone piles must have taken thousands of slaves many years to build, but so strong was the belief that the king's future life depended on such a structure that the whole wealth of Egypt was poured into the work. The noblemen, too, had tombs built for themselves, but these were smaller and less costly.

The Egyptians thought that a man would need everything in the next world that he needed in this, so along with statues of the man who had

7

Models of Brewers' and Bakers' Shops,
from a Tomb of the 11th Dynasty

The photographs on this page are from The Metropolitan Museum of Art, Museum Excavations, 1919–20; Rogers Fund, supplemented by contribution of Edward S. Harkness

Models of a Cattle Stable,
from a Tomb of the 11th Dynasty

Model of a Pleasure Boat,
from a Tomb of the 11th Dynasty

From the British Museum, reproduced in Egyptian Tomb Paintings, by courtesy of Faber and Faber, Ltd.

Jewelers at Work, from a Tomb of the 18th Dynasty

passed away were placed figurines of his servants doing everything for him they had done in life or would have to do for him after death. We have found miniature stables full of fattened cattle, and brewers' and bakers' shops with figures pouring beer and kneading bread, weavers' shops with little women at the loom, and granaries with figurines grinding flour. Necessary, too, were little boats manned by tiny seamen waiting to sail their masters down the Nile to the "land of the blessed."

The walls of the passages and rooms inside the tombs, and the walls and columns of the temples and palaces that have been discovered, are covered with pictures of everyday life. We see the Egyptians fishing, hunting, and harvesting, working at their trades, eating, dancing, singing, and playing at games and sports. Look, for example, at the painting of jewelers at work, and at the laughing and chatting ladies who are guests and musicians at a party. No subject was too unimportant to delight

Sculptors at Work on a Statue, from a Tomb of the 18th Dynasty

The Metropolitan Museum of Art

*Guests and Musicians,
from a Chapel of the
18th Dynasty*

these people; we have found pictures of men carving a statue and even waiting to be clipped in a barber's shop! And so it is that with the help of these we can imagine their sunny lives.

But how peculiar these dark people in their simple dress and great black wigs look to us. Surely they could not have been as stiff and rigid and as similar to one another as they seem in their pictures. And indeed, they were not. The artist did not try to make his figures appear true to life.

The Egyptians felt that for a statue to represent a certain man, it need merely have all the features of that man at his best. Anything that was not pleasant, such as a wrinkle or wart, and any kind of expression, as for example a smile, was left out.

Statues were generally either seated, with hands on knees, or standing, with the left leg forward and arms stiffly at the sides, as we can see when we look at the figures of Queen Hatshepsut and King Amenhotep III of the Eighteenth Dynasty.

Barber at Work,
from a Tomb of the 18th Dynasty

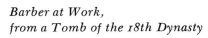

Statue of Queen Hatshepsut, 18th Dynasty   Statue of Amenhotep III, 18th Dynasty

Head of Queen Nefertiti, 18th Dynasty

Artisans at Work, from a Tomb of the 18th Dynasty

In paintings we see uncomfortable-looking figures with heads in profile, shoulders as seen from the front, and legs as seen from the side, for the Egyptians found it difficult to draw a side view of shoulders or a front view of a face. Strangely too, women were always painted a lighter color than men, and important people were made much larger than those around them. Look, for example, at the picture of artisans at work. The overseer is twice the size of any of the workmen. These set ways of showing a figure, unlifelike though they may be, were established, and changed very little. When this happens to the art of a people, we say that their painting or sculpture is "stylized." In fact, painting for the Egyptians was just another way of telling a story, and so little did they worry about showing things as they saw them that when they painted a man polishing a string of beads, as in the picture of the jeweler's workshop, they painted all the strings he had already polished in rows,

one on top of another, in front of him!

Did the Egyptians prefer to paint and sculpt this way? Could they make nothing more true to life? The rule of one brilliant young Pharaoh of the Eighteenth Dynasty, named Akhenaten, proves that they could. Born the son of the great warrior Amenhotep III, whose statue we have seen, and heir to the throne of Egypt, this young king tried from the very start to break all the rigid old customs that had held his country for 1,500 years. He wanted art more true to life, and the statues of Akhenaten himself, with his long jaw and heavy lips, are not at all flattering, but we can see the true beauty of his wife, Nefertiti. How different this head is from the statue of her father-in-law, carved in the stiff manner that had been used for so many centuries.

Unfortunately, after Akhenaten's death, the Egyptians returned to their old ways, and there was little change for another 1,500 years.

III

Art in King Minos' Labyrinth

The ancient Greeks used to tell a strange story about Crete, the large island in the Mediterranean to the south of Greece. They said that this island was once ruled by a king named Minos, who kept a monster called the Minotaur, half man and half bull, imprisoned in a huge maze called the Labyrinth. The tale went that the Greeks of the city of Athens had to send seven girls and seven young men every seven years to be sacrificed to the beast. One year Theseus, the son of the king of Athens, was sent along with the other young people, and he swore he would slay the Minotaur. This was doubly difficult, for even if he were successful, Theseus would surely get lost in the great maze of the Labyrinth and never be able to find his way out. Happily, though, Ariadne, the daughter of King Minos, fell in love with the handsome hero and determined to help him. And she had a very bright idea. The night before the fourteen Athenians were to be sacrificed, she and Theseus stole to the Labyrinth. Ariadne brought with her a ball of string. She told Theseus to take one end of the

string with him, and she herself held the ball while he sought the Minotaur. So it was that when he had slain the beast, he was able to follow the string and find his way out of the Labyrinth to freedom.

The ancient Greeks themselves knew of no trace of King Minos or the Labyrinth, and so it was thought for many centuries that this extraordinary tale was make-believe. And then, only about seventy-five years ago, an archaeologist named Schliemann decided to dig for remains of an ancient civilization on the island of Crete, and to the astonishment of the world, his followers discovered, not many feet below the surface of the land, the ruins of a great palace with many winding passages and small rooms. The Labyrinth! Of course, the fact that such a palace was found does not prove that King Minos actually lived, or that he kept a monster imprisoned in it, but it does prove that there were once, from about 2000 to 1200 B.C., wealthy kings who ruled the people on this island and who lived for many generations in a palace that might well have seemed to be a maze

Giraudon

Blue Bird Rising from Rocks, from Knossos

Throne Room, from the Palace of Minos at Knossos

to early Greek travelers. These kings might even have defeated the Athenians and demanded tribute every seven years. And perhaps one year a young prince called Theseus did come. All this we will never know.

What is important to us is that the Cretans covered the walls of this palace, and of others that we have found since, with colorful paintings, not for the sake of the dead, but to amuse the living. And what a sight these scenes are—full of free, swirling lines. The Cretans loved to paint animals and flowers, and their pictures were at the same time true to life and yet very imaginative. Look at the picture of a blue bird rising from rocks, with wild roses and lilies. What a free and

graceful decoration this is! On the walls of the throne room itself in this great palace are pictured huge seated griffins, imaginary animals, against a background of tall papyrus plants and billowing stripes of colors. What could be more fanciful? Strangest of all, there are many pictures of bulls, and in one we see something like a remarkable bullfight, with three young people doing somersaults over the animal's back. Could this have anything to do with the tale of the Minotaur?

The Cretans painted figures of people as well as animals, and there are many pictures of pretty ladies with curly black hair, like the painting of the girl called *The Parisian* because of her saucy expression, and tall handsome men, such as *The*

Copy of Acrobats Leaping over a Bull, from the Palace of Minos at Knossos

Courtesy of the Fogg Museum, Harvard University

"The Parisian,"
from the Palace of Minos at Knossos

Priest-King. Like the Egyptians, they showed their figures in profile, and unfortunately, like the Egyptians, they had difficulty in representing the shoulders from a side view, and as a result the figures appear out of joint. As with the Egyptians too, the men in Cretan pictures are painted a darker color than the women. But how much freer and more graceful these figures seem than any of those from the tombs along the Nile.

The Cretans did not make large statues as the Egyptians did, but they did carve small figurines. One of the best of these is an ivory figure of a woman holding two snakes in her hands before her. Perhaps she was the goddess whom these people worshipped. As with so many things about the Cretans, we do not know, and we are only just beginning to learn to read their writing, so we must imagine their life as we see it in their pictures—bright and gay, and full of a love for animals and nature.

16

Cretan Snake Goddess

The Priest-King, from the Palace
of Minos at Knossos

IV

Art in the Palaces of the Heroes of Homer

Perhaps you have read the stories from the great poems of Homer, the *Iliad* and the *Odyssey*—how King Agamemnon set out to conquer Troy and bring back Helen, the wife of King Menelaus of Sparta, and how, with the help of the brave Achilles, he defeated Priam, the Trojan king. And then you may have read how another Greek hero, Odysseus, or Ulysses, as the Romans called him, was blown from his course when sailing back to Greece and his wife, Penelope, and had many adventures in strange foreign lands. The Greeks of later times knew these stories well, but they thought that, like the story of King Minos and the Labyrinth, they were invented by the poet who had first told them. Then, lo and behold, less than a century ago, the palaces of these very heroes were uncovered by the same Schliemann who later began to dig in Crete, and again what was thought to be fable turned out to be fact.

The Greeks of whom Homer wrote must have lived at the same time or shortly after the Cretans, and their style of art was very much the same. But there were some differences.

The palace at Mycenae is just the sort of great stronghold we might expect as the home of the staunch Agamemnon—surrounded by huge, thick walls hiding rich treasures of gold. Over the gate to the palace we find what we do not find in Crete —large sculpture. Here are two strong lions standing on either side of a column and haughtily defending the entrance. They are "in relief," which is to say that instead of standing completely free so that they can be seen on all sides, they are cut into the background.

Large sculpture was not the only difference, for these early Greeks were a more warlike people than the Cretans in their peaceful island home. The Mycenaeans loved pictures of hunts and battles, scenes we never see painted in Crete. And yet, the style is just as charming and their colors

18

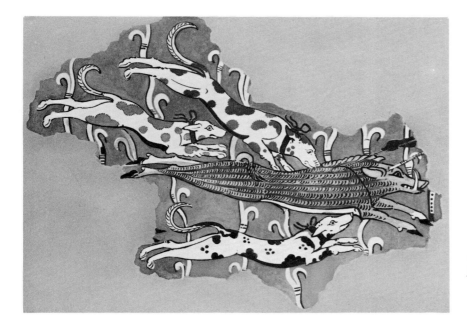

Boar Hunt,
from the Palace at Tiryns

even more fantastic. Look at the boar hunt from the palace at nearby Tiryns. The prey is being attacked by gay dogs with pink and green spots and ribbons around their necks! And look at the ladies driving a chariot. They are indeed pretty and cheerful cousins of *The Parisian* whom we saw in Crete.

Ladies Driving a Chariot,
from the Palace at Tiryns

Faille-Giraudon

The Lion Gate, from the Palace at Mycenae

V
Greek Art

Many people consider the ancient Greeks the greatest artists that ever lived, and it is their work we are going to look at next. These Greeks were the descendants of the Mycenaeans of whom I spoke in our last chapter, but the memory of their ancestors remained only in poetry and, as artists, the later Greeks had to learn from the very beginning.

We do not know who destroyed the Mycenaean palaces, but after they fell there was a long "Dark Age," by which we mean a time when there is not much art or writing and little record is kept of events. When the Greeks began to have these things again, we find them living in many separate towns, each one ruled by a group of nobles. These towns or cities were called city-states because each had a government of its own, and there was no large group of towns under one king as there had been in Egypt and Crete.

Greece is a rocky barren country with many bays and harbors, and so the ancient Greeks turned to the sea and became traders and fishermen. But

what is most important about the Greeks is that above all, they loved art and poetry and greatly admired skill in athletics. So it was that the city-states competed with one another not only in trade but also in the decorating of their cities with the most beautiful statues and paintings, in winning the most prizes at the great athletic meetings or "games" held every year, and in gaining the most praise at the drama festivals, where the plays of the greatest poets of each town were performed. This love of the beautiful motions of athletes and of great works of art and poetry was only part of the Greeks' one great love of beauty. In fact, the very words the Greeks used for "a gentleman"— *kalos k'agathos,* mean "a beautiful and good man."

The Greeks believed in a large family of gods who sat in golden palaces on Mount Olympus, eating a divine food called "ambrosia," drinking "nectar," and living the most agreeable kind of life imaginable. Zeus was the king of the gods and his wife, Hera, the queen, and the lesser gods and goddesses were his children. The Greeks thought that each of the gods ruled over a different part of human life. So, for example, Mars was the god of war, while Aphrodite was the goddess of love. These gods were like human beings in every way except that they were perfect in beauty, they could see great distances and move with great speed, and, above all, they lived forever. As most of the Greek works of art were made to decorate temples to the gods, the subjects were always either the gods themselves or scenes taken from the many beautiful and fascinating stories, or "myths" as they are called, that were told about them. Almost the only exceptions to this rule were statues of the athletes who had honored their city by winning in one of the "games," particularly the famous Olympic Games held every four years for competitors from all over Greece.

The first statues that the Greeks made were stiff and stylized like those of the Egyptians. The figures stood, facing forward, with their arms stiffly at their sides, or else sat in an equally stiff position. Their faces were wide-eyed and expressionless, their hair like a wig. But the Greeks, even in those early times (from about 750 B.C. to 500 B.C.), unlike the Egyptians, tried to show the bones and muscles of their figures beneath their clothing in a more natural way. They experi-

The Metropolitan Museum of Art

mented and they were not always successful, but still their statues became more and more lifelike. See, for example, *The Calf-Bearer,* a young man carrying a calf on his shoulders in a way that primitive herdsmen still do today. The sculptor had a true feeling for the shape of his subject's cheek and the muscles of his arms. And how soft and real the calf seems. And see the statue of a maiden found on the Acropolis. The fussy curls of her hair do not seem natural and the folds of her dress are too flat and regular. Yet, as we look at her, we can clearly see a form beneath the robe.

The Calf-Bearer, 6th Century B.C.

Black-Figured Vase: Theseus and the Minotaur, 6th Century B.C

Unfortunately, all Greek paintings have been lost, and so we must judge the Greeks' skill as painters from the decorations on their vases. In this early period, the Greeks found it easier to paint black figures on the natural red clay of the vase. Have you ever noticed how much easier it is to draw a silhouette than a complete figure with all its details? This was called the "black-figured style." See the vase painting of Theseus slaying the Minotaur. The painters faced the same problems as did the sculptors, in the same way. The detail is lovely, like the robe of the *Acropolis Maiden,* but although they form a beautiful design, the figures are shown only in profile and they are stiff and not quite true to life.

At the beginning of the fifth century, one of the most important campaigns in the history of the world took place, and it had a great effect on the history of art. To the east of Greece, in Asia Minor, the Persian Empire had grown to great strength under its kings Cyrus and Darius. The Greek historian Herodotus tells many stories of the rich court of these kings. Now Darius became jealous of the growing power of his neighbors, the Greeks, and wanted revenge for the aid they had given to the cities of Greeks in his own empire, and so he sent an expedition against them under his chief lieutenant. This campaign was a failure, for the Persian ships were wrecked off the coast of Greece. But Darius was determined to try again. This time he advanced with a great horde. He was beaten back by the men of Athens in their heroic defense on the plain of Marathon. From that time on, Athens was regarded as the first city-state in Greece. When Xerxes, Darius' son, came to the throne, he swore he would avenge his father and conquer Greece once and for all. He assembled the largest army that had ever been collected —over a million men, according to some reports— and to transport it he built a bridge of ships across the Hellespont, the neck of water separating

The Charioteer of Delphi, 5th Century B.C.

22

Head of the Charioteer of Delphi, 5th Century B.C.

already crowned and standing in his chariot, his eyes made of colored stones so that they flash with life. His hair is still wiglike, but his face is far rounder and more natural, and the features seem to be actually a part of it, and not merely put on by the artist. The figure is still facing straight forward and a bit stiff, but his proportions (the size of each part of the body in relation to the other parts) are true to life. And see how much more real the drapery appears, now that the folds are deep and rounded. A few years after this statue, Greek artists were able to create figures in every possible position. See, for example, the *Discus Thrower* by one of the first great sculptors known by name, Myron. The athlete is performing the tremendous twist of a thrower preparing to let go of his discus, or round stone slab, in a competition to see who can throw the farthest. The sculptor has made the motion seem so real that we feel we must move aside to keep from being struck by the discus when the thrower lets go. Myron was

The Discus Thrower, by Myron, 5th Century B.C.

Alinari–Art Reference Bureau

Greece from Asia Minor. With this huge force he crushed all before him and burned the Acropolis, the sacred hilltop fortress of Athens, with all its great buildings and sculpture. But, outnumbered as they were, the Greeks showed the spirit that made them the greatest people of the ancient world, and defeated Xerxes' fantastic army at the naval battle of Salamis (480 B.C.). By the end of that day, scarcely a man remained of what had been such a huge force at dawn, and Xerxes retreated to Persia in defeat. Greek culture and Greek art had been saved.

But there was much rebuilding to be done. The whole Acropolis of Athens had to be reconstructed and adorned with new statues. And, in the field of art, as in everything else, Athens took the lead.

Great strides were made. In the fifty years after the Battle of Salamis, Greek art developed to a height not equaled before or since. The first steps can be seen in a figure called the *Charioteer of Delphi,* a bronze statue made soon after the war. Here we see a victor in the chariot races, shown

also the sculptor of a beautiful and gently turning statue of Athena, the goddess of wisdom from whom Athens took its name. Notice how irregular, and therefore more natural, are the folds of Athena's robe compared with those of the *Charioteer of Delphi*. Athena is a warrior goddess, and she wears a helmet above one of the loveliest faces in Greek sculpture.

A few years later, the great sculptor Polyclitus showed a still fuller knowledge of how to represent the human body. Look at the head of his *Diadoumenos,* which means "Young Man Binding His Head with a Fillet." His hair is no longer wiglike but natural, his flesh seems softer and more real, and the pose of the whole figure is more relaxed. When we look at these works we must remember

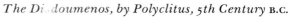

The Diadoumenos, by Polyclitus, 5th Century B.C.

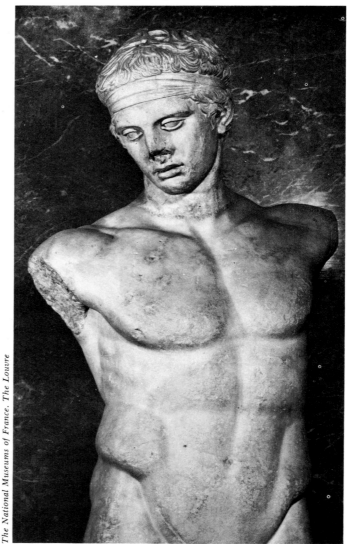

Statue of Athena, by Myron, 5th Century B.C.

The Three Fates from the Parthenon, by Phidias, 5th Century B.C.

that many of them have been injured and broken by time.

And now, around the middle of the fifth century, came the Golden Age, when art, architecture, and poetry reached their height. Pericles, the great democratic ruler of Athens, engaged the finest architects of the day to build the beautiful temple to Athena, called the Parthenon, on the Acropolis. Phidias, the greatest sculptor of the century, was called upon to decorate it. Now he made a huge statue of Athena, in helmet and armor, to be placed inside the temple. It was thirty-six feet high, with skin of ivory and robes of gold, and it became so famous for its beauty that people felt that the goddess herself could not have been more beautiful. But alas, this statue was destroyed in ancient times, so we must judge Phidias' genius from the other works on the Parthenon, and how magnificent these are! Look at

the *Three Fates,* the goddesses who spin the thread of life. We can almost feel the fragile, billowy drapery and at the same time we can see the perfect forms beneath. It is amazing to think that one man in his lifetime could have watched both the sculptor working on the *Acropolis Maiden* and Phidias working on his Parthenon figures!

We must remember when we look at these cool marble statues that they were originally painted in natural and lovely colors. They are white only because those colors have faded or rubbed off with age. In fact, all the great temples and public buildings of Athens were adorned with vivid colors so that the whole city was full of warmth and life.

In 431 B.C. came the deadly Peloponnesian War between Athens and Sparta, and by the end of the century, Athens was totally defeated, never again to regain her strength and grandeur. Still, art continued much as it had. In fact, figures became

25

Nike Fastening Her Sandal, 5th Century B.C.

Statue of Hermes, by Praxiteles, 4th Century, B.C.

softer and more graceful, and drapery still more delicate. Let us look at the relief of the *Nike,* or goddess of victory, stooping to fix her sandal. Her drapery seems so fine, it hardly looks as if it could have been made of cloth. See, too, the statue of the messenger of the gods, Hermes, by the fourth-century sculptor Praxiteles. It is said that when this statue was first unearthed, the discoverer sent a picture of it to a friend, an expert in ancient sculpture. The friend replied that he found the new statue most beautiful, but he wondered why the workmen had left a cloth hanging on the stump on which the figure is leaning. Needless to say, the "cloth" was in fact marble, and well over two thousand years old! How soft and real the hair and skin, too, appear, and with what a graceful gesture Hermes holds the infant Dionysus, who later became the god of wine. The same is true of the athlete's head of the same period. Compare this soft wistful face with the hard and noble lines of the head of the *Athena* by Myron of a century earlier. We would expect to meet with the face of the *Athena* on Mount Olympus, but this young man

is someone we might well meet on earth.

We can tell that the same improvements must have been made in painting, although we have no examples but those we see on vases. After the Persian War, vase painters began to draw their figures in outline on the red clay and then blacken in the background. This is called the "red-figured style," as the figures themselves appear in the natural red of the clay on which they were drawn. Let us look at a vase decorated with scenes from the Battle of Greeks and Amazons (a legendary nation of warrior women). The figures are almost as natural and graceful as those on the Parthenon, and they can be seen from every direction in every position. The artist has one problem, though, which he has not solved. He wants some figures to appear further back in the picture

Head of an Athlete, 4th Century B.C.

Red-Figured Vase: Battle of Greeks and Amazons, 5th Century B.C.

than others. This idea of distance in a flat painting is called "perspective." The painter of this vase has put the figure on the left and the spearman in the center, which are meant to appear behind the horse, on a higher level, as forms further back would appear to be, but he has not made the figures any smaller, so the effect of distance is lost. It was for later painters to solve this problem.

You may know the myth of Orpheus and Eurydice—how Orpheus played so sweetly on his lyre that he could charm the very beasts of the wood, and how, when his wife died, he followed her to the underworld, the land of departed souls, and won her back by soothing the unhappy spirits with his song. If we look at the fifth-century relief of Orpheus and Eurydice, united by the god Hermes, we can perhaps realize what is most moving about Greek art. See how Hermes, on the left,

is gently holding Eurydice by the hand, and how she is tenderly touching her husband's shoulder. There is not much motion, and very little expression on the faces of these figures, and yet we can feel the sadness and affection of the great myth, and all is beautiful and calm and noble.

Perhaps you have noticed that these statues and paintings are not only beautifully done, but always appear to be of beautiful people. When the Greek artist decided to portray a god or goddess, or even a mortal man, an athlete or a citizen of Athens, he did not choose some person he knew as a model, but rather tried to sculpt the most beautiful person he could imagine. Every line of the body, every feature of the face, had to be perfect. When an artist does this and portrays only the most perfect or "ideal" figure, we call it "idealization." Of all the artists in history, none idealized their subjects so much as the Greeks.

Hermes, Eurydice, and Orpheus, 5th Century B.C.

VI
Alexander Conquers the East

Around 334 B.C. another great historical event had an important effect on art. This was Alexander's conquest of the East. During the fourth century B.C., the city-states of Greece wasted their strength squabbling with one another, and the rugged and uneducated people of the land of Macedonia to the north of Greece gained power under their great king, Philip.

Philip's son, Alexander, proved to be a brilliant leader at an early age, and by the time he was thirty this handsome young man, who liked to be portrayed wearing the horns of a ram, had conquered most of the known world. He had marched his troops through the ancient kingdom of Persia and Afghanistan with its fabulous cities of gold. Over the high Kabul Pass to India and down into the Punjab to the shores of the Indus they went, and all the Oriental armies fell before them. No Europeans had ever before been so far. When Alexander died at the age of thirty-two, his generals became the rulers of the countries he had conquered, and they brought with them Greek

nobles for their courts, and Greek artists. So it was that at this time Greek art was spread throughout the Middle East. Now the most important Greek art might be produced at Alexandria in Egypt, or at Pergamon in Asia Minor, and no longer in Greece itself. Because of this it was called "Hellenistic" art, which means art in the style of the Hellenes (the word the Greeks used for their own people) .

But there were other changes as well. The Greek city-state was no longer important, and fewer great temples were being built. Artists were now called on to decorate private homes and gardens, and for this purpose they no longer needed to make statues of beautiful gods and athletes alone. Now sculptors tried to portray real people as they actually looked. Any subject would do, and they had the skill to try any subject. See for example the old marketwoman, a wrinkled hag shouting in anger at some passer-by. There is no "idealization" here. Children were a favorite subject. Look at the pudgy child with a goose, and the boy taking a

Child with a Goose, Hellenistic Period

thorn out of his foot. Nothing like this had been done before.

Along with the new way of showing people as they really looked, to decorate homes, came the idea of portraits. Alexander himself was among the first people to have a true portrait made, and he liked it so much that he took his favorite sculptor along with him on his campaigns. This artist, Lysippus by name, was famous for getting exactly the tilt of Alexander's head and the expression in his eyes. Now for the first time we see portraits that are true likenesses, not sparing a wrinkle to flatter the subject.

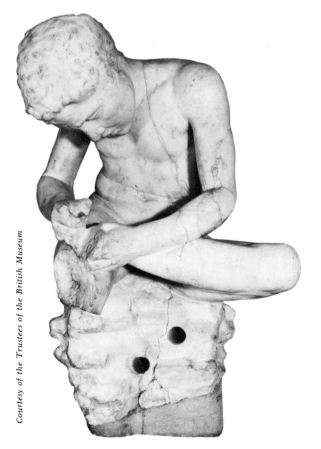

Old Marketwoman, 2nd Century B.C.

Boy Taking a Thorn out of His Foot, Hellenistic Period

Portrait Head of Alexander

Head of the Statue of Laocoön,
Hellenistic Period

Winged Victory of Samothrace,
Hellenistic Period

Detail of Alexander from the Battle of Issus,
Roman Copy of a Greek Painting
of the Hellenistic Period

Now, too, the sculptors began showing emotion on the faces of their figures. Joy, pain, or sorrow brought statues to life. What could be more woeful than the face of Laocoön? He has told the Trojans not to allow the giant horse left by the Greeks into their city, and Poseidon, the god of the sea, has sent serpents to destroy him and his sons.

One of the finest works of this period is the famous *Winged Victory*. This lovely headless figure of a goddess of victory was found on the island of Samothrace, and her setting was very strange indeed. She was made to appear to be just landing on the prow of a ship made of stone. To complete the picture, a pool of water was placed in front of the ship's prow to make it seem to be at sea. There was no experiment the Hellenistic sculptor would not try.

Many of the greatest paintings of the ancient world date from this period. These works, which were generally murals painted on the walls of private homes and public buildings, have all disappeared with the ages. Fortunately, though, there are some later Roman wall paintings that are copies of these, and from them we can judge what the Hellenistic models were like. One example is *The Battle of Issus*. Here we see the Greeks under Alexander meeting the Persians under Darius, the the descendant of the king who was defeated at Salamis. Here is the scramble of battle, figures shown at every angle, and a whirl of action as Alexander wins one of the greatest victories of his campaign. But notice, all the figures are on one level. There is no deep background, and little perspective.

Although it appears to be a painting, this Roman work is actually a "mosaic." A mosaic is a picture made of many tiny pieces of colored stone set in plaster. If you look at it from close at hand, you can see the many little stones, but at a distance, they blend together and the picture looks like a painting. Mosaics were very popular in Hellenistic and Roman times.

So it was that the art of a few cities on the small peninsula of Greece became the art of the whole ancient world, and eventually the basis of all the art we know in Europe and America today.

The Battle of Issus, Roman Copy of a Greek Painting of the Hellenistic Period

VII

Rome Rules the World and Adopts Greek Art

The next great event in the history of the world and the history of art was the rise of Rome and the conquest of Europe by Roman armies.

When we think of Rome we think of a great city of magnificent marble temples and public buildings. We think of grave and worthy senators in flowing togas (this was the name they gave to the particular kind of draped robe they wore), and emperors who lived in great luxury. The life we imagine is very much like that of the Greeks in dress and in every form of art. Yet the history books tell us that the Romans were originally simple tribesmen who lived on the River Tiber in central Italy, far from Greece, and who spoke Latin. Why, then, should this be so?

There are many reasons why, in everything and particularly in art, the Romans took the Greeks as their teachers. To begin with, in the eighth century B.C. there were colonies of Greeks who came to set up towns, like the Greek city-states, in southern Italy. When the Latin tribes who lived in the city of Rome grew to strength and began

to conquer the other peoples of Italy, they met with these Greeks, whose life was much easier than their own and who possessed beautiful works of art. The Romans had taken the alphabet with which these people wrote and used it to write their own language; they adopted their dress, and copied their architecture. Moreover, they discovered that their own gods were just like the gods of the Greeks. Their Jupiter, king of the gods, was like Zeus, and his wife, Juno, like Hera. Their Venus, goddess of love, was like Aphrodite, and their Mars, the god of war, was like Ares. If this was so, they reasoned, then the many lovely myths about the Greek gods must be about their own gods as well. So they took for their own the literature and art of Greece that depicted such gods.

In the third century B.C., these Romans seized the very Greek cities in southern Italy from which they had learned so many things, and soon they began to look beyond Italy for more territory. This new, strong nation conquered the old lands around the Mediterranean one by one. First Rome

Portrait of the Emperor Augustus, 1st Century B.C.

their ancestors, and Roman artists were skilled at getting likenesses. When Rome came to rule many distant lands, it was important for the newly conquered peoples to know and revere the men who ruled them from afar, and so there were many great portraits of emperors. See the statue of Augustus, for example. Who could fail to admire the grandeur and dignity of such a ruler? The Romans were equally good at showing all the ages of man. Look at the deeply lined and trouble-worn face of Cicero, the patriot who put down the rebellion of Cataline, and at the powerful head of the Emperor Caracalla.

Portrait Head of Cicero, 1st Century B.C.

Portrait Head of the Emperor Caracalla, 3rd Century A.D.

defeated Carthage, her rival in North Africa, then Greece itself, worn out by the many wars between the city-states, and then Egypt and parts of ancient Persia. The conquerors brought home with them thousands of the finest statues they found in Greece, and these became the admiration of all Rome. They were set up in temples, squares, and private homes. So it was that Roman artists imitated the Greeks in every way they could, and Roman art became in many ways a continuation of Greek art. In fact, because they were so much alike, we speak of "Classical art," which means both Roman and Greek art together.

In some ways the Romans even excelled the Greeks in art. Portraits were of great importance to them. It was the tradition for people who were proud of their families to keep portrait busts of

Base of Trajan's Column, 2nd Century A.D.

Unlike the Greeks, the Romans wanted to decorate their public buildings with scenes of their conquests in relief. They wanted to tell the story of a military campaign or some public event, showing one scene after the next, so that anyone could tell the whole story by looking at the episodes one after another. Trajan set up a great column in Rome relating his conquests in Germany, with the scenes winding in a spiral up the column from the bottom to the top. We see his troops marching, crossing a river, and attacking a town, and from the details we can get a very good idea of what Roman warfare was like.

And how skilled the Romans were at the most delicate detail. Look at the relief of priests and members of the Emperor's family from the *Altar*

Relief from the Altar of Peace, 1st Century B.C.

Marble Vase with Dancing Figures, Roman Period

of Peace that Augustus set up in honor of the power of Rome that was to end all wars. How perfectly the hair and drapery of the figures have been modeled! Here we see portraits of Augustus (in the center) and his family, with little Lucius Caesar clinging nervously to his grandfather's toga. And look at the graceful dancers done in relief on a marble vase of the same period. We can almost hear the soft music the piper is playing.

There are very few Greek wall paintings that have not been destroyed by time, but we have many by Roman artists because of the strange fate of Pompeii. In the days of ancient Rome, Pompeii was a sunny resort town where the Romans went to have a pleasant vacation by the seaside. August 24, A.D. 79, was a warm day like any other, except that it was a holiday, and many of the people of Pompeii had gone to watch the games in the local arena. Suddenly the nearby mountain of Vesuvius began to rumble. There was a flash of fire and the sky grew as dark as night, for, unknown to the Romans, Vesuvius was really an active volcano and now it was erupting. Many people fled, but

the whole town of Pompeii and its neighbor, Herculaneum, were buried in ashes and lava, melted rock that poured down the sides of the mountain. When the ashes and lava cooled and hardened, the towns had so completely disappeared beneath that one would think they had never been there at all.

Pompeii and Herculaneum remained buried for almost two thousand years, but in the last century archaeologists began digging where Pompeii once lay and beneath the rock they found the whole town as it had been on that dreadful day two thousand years before, for when the people of Pompeii had fled, they had left everything behind them. They found bakers' shops with loaves of bread still in the oven, grocery stores with food still on the counter, and shops selling all kinds of things. On the walls of houses were scribbled messages we might find in any town today— "Gaius loves Idaia," "Beware of the Dog," "Vote for Fronto." And what is most important for the history of art, the archaeologists found that the walls of many of the rooms in the lovely private homes, or villas, as the Romans called their coun-

*Wall Painting of a Garden Scene,
1st Century* B.C.

From The Art of Rome and Her Empire, ©Holle Verlag G.m.b.H., Baden-Baden, Germany, 1963

Wall Painting of an Architectural Scene,
1st Century A.D.

try houses, were covered with beautiful paintings.

And what paintings! Roman painters could portray anything in the most true-to-life way and they decorated the walls of many homes all over Italy with colorful scenes. Sometimes they tried to make the wall seem like one big window, with a view of a street or an architectural scene or a beautiful landscape—a formal garden or a mountainside. And they often painted figures, such as the *Lady Playing a Cithara,* a woman playing an ancient string instrument, while a little girl peeks

over the back of her chair. The Roman painter had only two problems. One was that his perspective was such that it is not always possible to tell how far away an object is meant to be. Notice the strange form of the chair on which the cithara player is sitting. Although it is not seen from the side, both the front and back leg seem to be equally near us. The second problem was that though his figures were modeled and shaded, the artist did not paint a scene so that it would appear that light was coming from one direction only.

These problems were not solved for another thousand years.

In the middle of the first century B.C., Julius Caesar, the greatest of all the Roman generals, led his troops through France, which was then called Gaul. The Romans had already invaded parts of Spain, and in another hundred and fifty years they conquered most of Europe. Before the Romans came, these lands had been inhabited by wandering tribes who lived poorly, were constantly fighting one another, and had little art of their own. These people fought the Roman invaders bravely, but when they were defeated, most of them settled down and accepted the rule of Rome. And how did the Romans rule? By setting up permanent camps for their soldiers and sending groups, or colonies, of their own people to live among the defeated tribesmen. These Romans brought with them their own art, the art they had learned from the Greeks, and the natives of the lands to which they went learned it from them. So it was that by the second century A.D., many artists in Gaul or Spain were making statues and paintings very like the works of Phidias or Polyclitus, produced in Athens five hundred years before. Classical art had become the art of Europe.

Wall Painting of a Lady Playing a Cithara, 1st Century B.C.

The Metropolitan Museum of Art, Rogers Fund, 1903

39

VIII

The Fall of Rome, Byzantium, and the Dark Ages

After the conquest of Europe, the Roman world enjoyed two hundred years of peace, called the *Pax Romana* (Roman Peace). But all was not well. The people living on the borders were constantly being attacked by "barbarians," groups of primitive tribesmen who wandered about in Germany and in the vast plains between Europe and Asia, and who envied the wealth of those who lived within the Roman Empire. What is more, in days when transportation and communication were slow, it was difficult for the Romans to rule such a far-flung domain. After a long succession of weak emperors, the government fell into confusion and was no longer able to send armies to defend its frontiers. Soon it ceased to have enough authority to keep the law within its borders, and the Empire began to fall apart, with the large landowners in each small town taking more and more power for themselves.

At the beginning of this time of strife, the people of Europe had no one strong faith to cling to. They no longer believed in the gods of the Roman state, and they needed another religion to

take its place. Christianity came to answer this need. In the first century A.D., the teachings of Jesus of Nazareth, who was one of the Jewish people that lived in Palestine and believed in one God, were spread throughout Europe and Asia Minor by his followers. Jesus had been crucified, or put to death by being nailed to a cross, by the Romans for his teachings, but his belief in one merciful God who was above the Roman state or any other earthly rule spread quickly among the troubled peoples of the Empire. At first the holders of this faith were treated as their leader had been. It is said that in order to put down the new religion that challenged the authority of the state, the Emperor Nero had the Christians thrown to lions in the arenas to amuse the crowds on holidays. All the same, the new belief took a stronger and stronger hold on the people, until in the fourth century, one of the emperors, Constantine I, became a Christian himself and made Christianity the religion of the state, thus bringing about the conversion of the whole Roman Empire.

Constantine established a new capital for the

40

Scene from the Life of Christ on a Late Roman Sarcophagus

Empire, named Constantinople after himself, on the site of the Greek city of Byzantium. He left Rome and set up his rule in this city far to the east, on the straits of the Bosphorus where Europe meets Asia. Constantinople, however, was too far away to rule the western part of the Empire, which had spread as far as France and Spain, and so, after years of warfare with many generals struggling for the title of Emperor, the Roman Empire split in two, one emperor ruling the eastern half with its capital at Constantinople, and another ruling the western half with its capital at Rome.

Meanwhile, what was happening to art? In the days of confusion the state no longer ordered artists to ornament magnificent monuments as before, and there were fewer fine homes decorated with beautiful wall paintings. Less attention was paid to art altogether, and artists began to show less and less skill. See, for example, the relief on a Roman "sarcophagus," or coffin, of the period, showing a scene from the life of Christ. Figures became flat and stiff, their positions became awkward, and artists were no longer able to portray anatomy correctly. The most important change of all was that with the coming of Christianity art had a new purpose. Fewer and fewer private people could afford works of art, and there were, of course, no more temples of the gods of Olympus to decorate. But the "Fathers of the Church" (by which we mean the leaders who organized Christian worship) felt it was important to decorate churches with pictures of scenes from the Bible,

to explain Christ's teachings to those who could not read and to be a constant reminder of them for those who could. Pope Gregory the Great, who was head of the Church at the end of the sixth century A.D., said that "painting can do for the illiterate [those who cannot read] what writing does for those who can read." Again, as in ancient Egypt, the telling of a story became all-important in art, while it was less and less important for the artist's figures to be true to life.

As we might expect, art in the eastern part of the Empire differed greatly from that in the West. In Constantinople, or Byzantium, as it was still called, the court of the Emperor took on the richness and splendor of the Orient, for there was constant trade with the East and the Byzantines copied the ways of the nearby Persian Empire. Byzantine artists never even tried to recapture the realism of Greek or Roman art, but made works famous for their rich color and lavish use of gold.

See, for example, the illustration of *The Martyrdom of Saint Autonomos*. The figures are flat and incorrectly drawn and the artist has no idea of perspective, so that the executioner seems to be in mid-air rather than on the hill behind the saint. Notice, too, that no attempt has been made to suggest depth. The scene is merely painted against a flat surface of brilliant gold. But the story is clearly told, for that is what really mattered to the artist. There can be no doubt that the executioner is about to cruelly kill the un-

μαρτυριον τοῦ

ἁγίου Καὶ ἐν δο

ξου μάρτυρος αὑ

τον ὁλου· ✝

The Martyrdom of Saint Autonomos,
Byzantine, 12th Century

happy saint—and how vivid the colors are, the bright blues and reds and greens; above all, what an attractive design the entire picture makes!

Mosaics were a favorite form of decoration in Byzantium. They were much more brilliant and impressive than those that decorated Roman houses, for they were made of chips of brilliantly colored glass rather than marble. We can get some idea of what they were like from the mosaic of the Empress Theodora and her train from the church of San Vitale in Ravenna, the Italian stronghold of the Byzantines. Of course, we must try to imagine the magnificence of the flashing gold and colored glass of which it is made. Theodora had been an actress, the daughter of a bear feeder in the circus, and her marriage to the Emperor Justinian caused a great scandal. But she became a powerful and intelligent ruler, and I think we can see some of her strength, and her beauty, for which she was so famous, in the huge commanding eyes we see here.

In Byzantium, as throughout the Christian world at this time, the chief subjects for works of art were scenes and persons from the Bible. As these were considered very sacred, artists were allowed to represent them in only a few set ways—

42

Mosaic of the Empress Theodora and Attendants, Byzantine, 6th Century

Enthroned Madonna and Child, Byzantine, 13th Century

such as, for example, the *Enthroned Madonna*, which is a picture of Mary, the mother of Christ, seen as she often is, in a blue robe, with the infant Jesus on her knees. For centuries one artist copied another in painting such "icons," or likenesses of saints and of characters from the Bible. Thus the art of Byzantium did not change until the city was captured by the Turks, invaders from the East, in 1453, over a thousand years after its founding.

Meanwhile, things were going very differently in the western half of the old Roman Empire. Its frontiers collapsed completely, and Italy was invaded again and again by hordes of barbarians: Huns, Goths, Vandals, and many more. The government at Rome ceased to have any power and each local landlord took upon himself the rule and protection of his weaker neighbors. This brought about what is called the "feudal system," with many lords of equal strength competing with one another and ruling over freemen, called villeins, who tilled their land in return for military protection, and serfs, who were like peasant slaves, the property of the nobles for whom they worked. The barbarian invaders soon settled down in the lands they conquered, bringing new languages and customs with them. Fewer and fewer people had any education, until reading and writing were almost forgotten. As for art, there was almost none to speak of. For these reasons, this period is often referred to as "the Dark Ages."

What art and learning continued in Europe was kept up by the Church, which was the only authority that was obeyed throughout Europe at this time, for all the barbarians had been converted to Christianity. The Church Fathers were often great scholars and writers, and the monks, the members of the religious orders, spent their lives quietly in monasteries, away from the everyday world, where they prayed and worked laboriously at copying by hand the Bible and the writings of Greek and Roman authors. Such manuscripts, or handwritten copies, were decorated with tiny pictures often meant as illustrations of the text. These decorations, which were called "illuminations" because they "lit up" the writings, brightening them and making them clear, were carefully and lavishly done, even though the pictures were often designed simply to ornament the first letter of a sentence. See, for example, the singing monks decorating the letter C at the beginning of a page from a thirteenth-century English manuscript. The C here is the first letter of the Latin word *cantate,* meaning "sing." Books were rare and very valuable, and the monks meant their work to last for a long time. It was in the illumination of these manuscripts that a knowledge of ancient art was kept alive, for it was the custom to circulate from one monastery to another "pattern books" which gave a ready guide as to how particular figures and stories could be represented in a way that everyone would recognize.

Singing Monks,
from an Illuminated Manuscript,
English, 13th Century

IX

Medieval Art

The word "medieval" means literally, having to do with a "Middle Age," and by this we mean the many centuries between the fall of the Roman Empire and the Renaissance, the age of the rebirth of Classical culture. At the beginning of this "medieval" period, the only kind of art that really flourished outside of the monasteries was the native art of the barbarian tribes. It is mainly from objects such as jewelry and metalwork dug up by archaeologists that we have to form our idea of what this barbarian art was like. Certainly it was very varied and lively at all times. The barbarian peoples were fond of crisscrossing and interlacing patterns of fine lines and colors, and they often worked into these designs the figures of beasts that were omens of all sorts in their own pre-Christian religion.

On Christmas Day in the year 800, Charlemagne had placed on his head the crown of the Roman Empire. This great monarch had subdued many of the tribes that were disturbing Europe, and converted to Christianity those who were not

yet Christian. He now felt he could try to rebuild the Roman Empire in Europe, and to control his newly won lands he experimented with many systems of government the Romans had used. He also encouraged the monasteries to grow, and to show more of an interest in Classical learning. Because it tried to bring back the spirit of Classical Rome, the art of the centuries that followed Charlemagne is called "Romanesque."

While Charlemagne remained alive, many of the changes he had hoped for came to pass, so great was his own authority and power. But after his death, his lands were split up between his heirs who fought with one another, and all his dreams of a new Roman Empire came to naught. His influence on art remained, but because his lands were split up, Romanesque art varies greatly from place to place.

Above all, people continued to live under the feudal system, and the Church was still the center that spread ideas about painting and sculpture and architecture from country to country. It was responsible for the building of countless new churches and monasteries as centers of worship, and for new ideas in architecture whereby these could be made handsomer and more uplifting for the soul, to remind one of heavenly things. It became the ambition of every true Christian to visit in his lifetime one shrine where the remains of a famous saint were kept. As a result, many pilgrimages were organized each year—the most popular were to the tomb of Saint James in Spain, to that of Saint Peter in Rome, and to the Church of the Holy Sepulcher (or tomb) in Jerusalem. This meant that churches had to be enlarged to receive the pilgrims, guesthouses had to be put up for them to stay in, and passages (ambulatories) built around the choirs and apses of the churches, so visitors could come near to the shrines without disturbing the ceremonies that were in progress. Monasteries and whole new towns sprang up along the roads that the pilgrims took. Music and rich new vestments made the church services more beautiful to hear and watch. Plays telling Bible stories, called mystery plays, were performed on special occasions, and the clergy themselves were always ready to explain questions of religion to those who did not know or understand.

Inside the monasteries, some monks busied themselves with the illumination of manuscripts, as we have already seen; others were sculptors highly skilled at working with stone and bronze and precious metals to decorate the interiors of churches. Each craftsman was really a specialist: one might specialize in the painting of figures, another in the modeling of little animals crawling through branches and leaves on the stem of a tall candlestick.

See, for example, part of an ivory carving of the Nativity, or birth of Christ, in the Romanesque style. It is from twelfth-century Germany, and was perhaps made in just such a monastic art-center as I have told you about. Anyone who knew the story of the birth of Christ from studying his Bible would expect to find represented in the relief all the things that he had read about there: the animals that were in the stable where Christ was born, the swaddling clothes in which the Babe was wrap-

ped, and Saint Joseph watching beside the crib. Sure enough, all these things are here, and the artist has been very careful to show them in the traditional way they had been shown for many centuries. It was traditional, for instance, to show Saint Joseph, whom they thought of as a tired old man, sitting down and resting his head on one arm. You may think that the figure of Saint Joseph is rather awkward and clumsy, but you must remember that another thing that mattered greatly to the artist was that each figure should wear a proper expression. The right expression for Saint Joseph in this case is one of humble wonder, and hence the face, upon which these feelings are expressed, has come out too large for the body that belongs with it.

You may notice too that as Charlemagne had planned, much attention has been paid to Roman art. Saint Joseph wears something quite like a Roman toga, or draped garment, and the crib looks rather like a Roman "sarcophagus," or coffin. It is interesting that you can see places on Saint Joseph's robe where the craftsman has traced the design for his relief from a sketch by punching holes through it and into the ivory behind it with a special tool. The animals look out through round-topped windows like those round-topped windows and arches used in the Romanesque style of architecture—and all these forms of architecture go back to those used by the Romans themselves for their forts and theaters.

The Romanesque period was followed, around the year 1200, by what we call the "Gothic" period. This new age was named after the Goths, one of the tribes of barbarians who had come many years before from the North, because its style of art and architecture began in the North. But the tribes that had been plundering Europe had long since settled down, and life was becoming easier and more prosperous.

The Church was stronger than ever, and with its new wealth it built huge cathedrals, the seats or headquarters of the bishops, higher officers of the Church, in the towns that were now becoming more important.

The Gothic style of architecture is tall, thin, and

pointed. Its soaring towers and arches carry the eye and the spirit towards heaven. Gothic cathedrals are rich with stained-glass windows that glow like jewels as the light pours in, and rich also with many other kinds of ornament.

Let us look at one part of a huge group of sculpture designed in the thirteenth century to decorate a doorway of the Cathedral of Reims in France. The size of this colossal cathedral—where Joan of Arc placed the crown of France on the head of the Dauphin—shows how much wealthier the people were becoming, and how very important their religion and the Church were to them.

Notice in our picture the rich decoration of the tops of the columns behind the figures' heads. To match the soaring lines of the cathedral, the figures themselves are tall and elongated. But the attention paid to the modeling of the arms and legs beneath the drapery tells us that the sculptors and stonemasons—for they were no longer necessarily monks—who worked here had looked carefully at nature and were beginning to try to portray things more as they really saw them.

On the left side you see the Annunciation—the Angel Gabriel coming to Mary to tell her that Christ is going to be born, and on the right the

Ivory Carving of the Nativity, German, 12th Century

Sculpture from a Doorway of the Cathedral of Reims, French, 13th Century

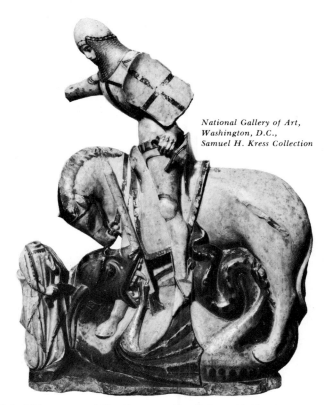

Saint George and the Dragon, English, 15th Century

Visitation, or Mary's visit to her cousin Elizabeth. Each figure stands on its own separate pedestal, but the two groups are clearly separated by the way in which the figures turn towards each other. The Angel Gabriel has a lively and smiling face, but Mary is more solemn, while Elizabeth has the lines of old age above her mouth. Many parts of the sculpture have been damaged by the wear and tear of the centuries, and Gabriel has lost one wing, but the detail of the feathers on the wing that remains shows us what fine craftsmen the Gothic sculptors were.

There were many figures of saints inside the churches and cathedrals as well. Look at the early fifteenth-century English statue of Saint George and the Dragon. There is a legend that Saint George slew a dragon to rescue a fair maiden, and here we see all the actors in the drama. The little figure on the left is the maiden, and the dragon is being crushed under the hoofs of Saint George's horse. How very like an illustration to a fairy tale this seems! We must remember that this was the age when fairy tales were told, and the world in which they might have happened.

And now see the tomb in Southwark Cathedral in London of an English poet called John Gower, who was buried there soon after 1400. On the coffin is a figure representing the poet at rest, all cast

in metal, with his hands clasped together in prayer. The canopy overhead gives a very good idea of what the Gothic style of architecture is like: notice how the arches come to a point at the top and how the structure is filled in with thin but firm carved work that curls in circles. Notice too the important details of the books under the poet's head—showing that he was a writer—and of the little lion crouching at his feet, which stands for the forces of evil that he trod down in his lifetime.

John Gower wrote for the educated landlords and gentlemen of his day, not for church folk. By this time the court and the nobles had begun to read and become interested in books, and so new kinds of illuminated manuscripts were produced which were owned and studied by private persons: little psalters, or prayerbooks, lives of the saints, and "Books of the Hours," which are manuals for a person's private prayers and devotions. In these books religious subjects are depicted just as they were in the great Bibles of the Romanesque period. But into the margins of the pages, where the artists let their fancy run free, there creep all sorts of little extra scenes and figures that are taken from everyday life or illustrate well-known romantic poems that were not at all on religious

The John Gower Tomb, Southwark Cathedral, English, 15th Century

Border of an Illuminated Manuscript, French, 15th Century

subjects. Here you find the wonderful leaves and petals of roses and lilies and other flowers, and monkeys sporting in the boughs of trees. You find court jesters and wandering minstrels and knights on horseback, and in other places there will be dragons and birds and all kinds of amusing delights of this sort. This drawing of scenes in the margins of books was called, of all things, "baboonerie," which is French for "monkey business." In other words, artists had started to look at the world around them again, instead of just at pattern books.

It was now that painting on a large scale and not merely for the decoration of books became important again. Handsome altarpieces had to be painted for the new cathedrals. Look at the picture, *The Calling of the Apostles Peter and Andrew,* by the Italian artist Duccio, who lived around 1300. Christ is bidding Peter and Andrew to leave their fishing and follow him, saying, "I will make you fishers of men." As in Byzantine paintings, there is almost no background, and the artist has used a great deal of gold. He is more interested in the lovely curling pattern of the edge of Christ's cloak than in making it seem true to life; but although the figures still seem stiff, see how gracefully they gesture to one another. Notice, too, how the faces are carefully modeled in light and dark tones, and how we can sense that there is a rounded figure beneath the robes, just as we can tell that the artist, here too, has begun to look at nature again. We shall see where this leads in the next period in our history of art, the "Renaissance."

The Calling of the Apostles Peter and Andrew, by Duccio (active 1278–1319)

X

What Does "The Renaissance" Mean?

And then, suddenly, Europe awoke from the quiet sleep of the Middle Ages. Around the end of the fourteenth and the beginning of the fifteenth century a great change came about. It had all started with the Crusades. In the eleventh and twelfth centuries, soldiers had gone out from all the corners of Europe to free the Holy Land from the Mohammedans, and when they came home, they had many a tale to tell of the luxuries of the East. They brought back with them beautiful silks, perfumes, and finely wrought gold. They brought back, too, a curiosity to know more about the world around them. They had seen strange foreign cities beyond the horizons they once knew, and they were anxious to search still further and find new routes to the East, whence came these new luxuries.

In the Middle Ages all of Europe was united under the Church. All educated people could speak and write the same language, Latin, and the style of art was everywhere the same. Artists traveled from place to place and copied one another. Their work was for the Church, and the Church was everywhere the same. But now there was a change. With their new interest in the world around them, people began to pay less heed to the teachings of their religion. They began to write in their own local languages, which they already spoke, and to look to their local rulers rather than to the fathers of the Church. This change is called the rise of "nationalism"—the feeling that the different peoples of Europe developed of belonging to separate nations, instead of owing allegiance to some neighboring lord and to the Church which united all the peoples of Europe. And with this sense of being part of a nation came local "schools" of art. When we say a "school" of art, we mean the style of art practiced in a certain place. Thus, when we say "the French school" of art, we mean the sort of painting and sculpture produced in France by artists who studied there even if they were not necessarily born in France.

With the desire for many new luxuries came the growth of trade and craftsmanship and with these came the growth of towns. In the Middle Ages life was simple and peasants lived in villages around the castles of their noblemen. They made what they needed at home, and the needs of the noblemen were filled by their own serfs. But now there were expert spinners and weavers, cabinetmakers and metalworkers, who sold their merchandise to all buyers, and for them a town was needed as a center to trade and sell their wares. These towns became centers for artists, too. The followers of a great master would come and live in the town where he worked, and it was the people of the towns that ordered work to be done. During the Middle Ages painters and sculptors had few other patrons than the Church. By "patron" is meant any person or group of people who pays an artist to do a piece of work, or commissions him, as we say. Now, although the Church was still the most important patron, there were many others. The wealthy nobles of the towns wanted paintings of themselves and their families. Portraiture had been forgotten during the Middle Ages, but now it was revived. Workers and tradesmen had formed guilds, private societies to aid the interests of members of a particular trade, such as furriers or blacksmiths or physicians. These guilds hired artists to decorate their meeting places, or guild halls, as they were called.

Above all, this was a great age of learning. Men were suddenly finding out about the world around them, and their curiosity and spirit of adventure led to the voyages of Marco Polo to the East and then of Columbus to the West. The printing press was invented and books no longer had to be laboriously copied by hand. The art of the illuminator began to die out, but there were more and more books, and people read and thought for themselves. They began to read the literature of ancient Greece and Rome, and this influenced them greatly. They wanted to read about their own life on earth and not about the "other world" of the Middle Ages, and so they tried to copy ancient writers. And, of course, they wanted all the earthly beauties of ancient Greece and Rome. They began digging up the remains of the buildings and statues of these great civilizations that had been buried for a thousand years, and artists tried to copy these

works, and to achieve their realism. It is from this return to Classical culture that we get the name "Renaissance," which in English means "Rebirth."

The Renaissance had its true beginning in Italy, and what an exciting and fascinating place it was in those days! Although the people spoke the same language throughout Italy, they were not united, as elsewhere, under one national king, but were divided into many city-states, like the ancient Greeks. These cities fought bloody wars between themselves, and within the towns the ruling families were always fighting one another for leadership. But of all the towns of Italy, none has a history more full of bloodshed and strife and great works of art than Florence.

Let us imagine Florence in the thirteenth century. The town was rich and bursting with life. Everyone, from the lowliest worker to the wealthiest nobleman, was competing with his neighbor, and everyone took sides in a great struggle between two parties for leadership. Those who favored the party of the Ghibellines wore white roses and white hats, cut their food sideways, and drank wine out of goblets, while those who were for the party of the Guelphs wore red roses and red hats, cut their food straight across, and drank their wine out of cups. There were constant street fights between the members of the two parties, and many a man who was important in either came to a mysterious end in the night.

But for all their violence, the Florentines loved art, and the artists of Florence were very important men. Like tradesmen they had a guild of their own. An artist was not only a painter and a sculptor; he was an architect as well. He was expected to be able to build the church or guild hall he decorated. And how did a child learn such a trade? There were no art schools. A young boy became an apprentice to a master painter as he would to a master shoemaker. He had to learn carpentering to be able to construct altarpieces and prepare panels, and he learned how to grind the color for paints. At this time, oil painting was not yet in use in Italy. Paintings were generally of two types: fresco, and tempera on wood. Frescoes are wall paintings in which the paint has been put on while

The Flight into Egypt, by Giotto (1266?–1337)

a coat of plaster on the wall is still wet. The paint seeps in, and when the plaster dries, the picture is part of the wall itself. For this sort of painting, an artist must work quickly and with a sure hand. If the picture was not to be on a wall but was to be a separate work, such as a portrait or altarpiece, it was generally painted on a wooden board or panel, in "tempera"—a sort of water color thickened with egg yolks.

The young apprentice had to master these skills, and, when he was not grinding colors, preparing panels, or doing little chores for his master, he would practice drawing. When he could draw and paint well enough, his master would let him do unimportant corners of the picture on which he himself was working. He might be allowed to paint a castle or a cloud in the background of a picture, or the flower in the hand of a lady. When he had learned enough to paint complete works of his own, he set up a studio, and took his own apprentices.

There is a story that one day a successful Florentine painter was walking through the meadows and hills near Florence, when he saw a little boy tending his sheep. The boy seemed very busy at something and when the painter came closer, he saw that the little fellow was drawing a picture of one of the sheep on a piece of slate. He stopped to look. Never had he seen such a drawing from the hand of a child! He asked the boy where he lived, and went to speak to his father. He told him that his son had a great talent and asked if he would consent to the boy's becoming an apprentice in his studio. The father was delighted at such an opportunity for his child and granted the artist's request. This little boy, whose name was Ambrogiotto, or Giotto for short, as he was later called, was his master's most successful pupil, and when he grew up, he was the first painter to bring realism to the flat although decorative painting of the Middle Ages. The Renaissance in painting began with Giotto (1266?–1337).

Men, as I have said, were beginning to look for the realistic representation of human beings they saw in the Classical statues that were being unearthed. Giotto was the first artist to be able to breathe such life into his figures. See, for example, his painting of *The Flight into Egypt.* An angel has come to Mary and told her to flee with her child from Bethlehem, where King Herod intends to slay all infants under the age of two. The figures in this painting are solid and rounded. Their anatomy is not perfect, but they are more true to life than anything that had been painted before. Above all, see the expressions on their faces. They are not just images out of a pattern book, but a truly worried family. The artist knows how to make them seem to be alive and weighed down with heavy thoughts. But Giotto has not solved all the painter's problems. His figures are modeled and round, but each is separate on a flat background. There is no air around them and no depth in the pattern of hills behind them.

These problems were for later artists to solve, and for the next hundred years and more one great master after another followed in Giotto's footsteps. They studied perspective and anatomy until they could show the human body in any position, and objects at any distance from the eye of the beholder.

Look at *The Youthful David* by Andrea del Castagno (1420?–1457). Here we see the triumphant shepherd David standing over the head of the fallen giant Goliath, his hair and clothing fluttering in the wind. Almost every muscle is perfect, and we can well believe that he is striding forward with hand upraised. His clothes, too, really are blown by the wind—they are more than a mere pattern of decorative, curling lines. This picture was painted on a leather shield for display in a parade, which explains its unusual shape. Castagno was a man famous for his ferocious temper, who was known to strike those who didn't like his paintings (not an unusual thing in the boisterous days of the Renaissance), and I think we can see some of his angry and fiery nature here. See, too, the painting of *Tobias and the Angel* by Filippino Lippi (1457?–1504). The story goes that Tobias' father was blind, and Tobias was such a good son that one day the Angel Gabriel came to him when he was fishing and said he would make an ointment from the bones of the fish that would cure

The Youthful David,
by Andrea del Castagno
(1420?–1457)

Tobias and the Angel, by Filippino Lippi (1457?–1504)

his father's blindness. Here we see Tobias, carrying his fish and walking with the angel, who holds the jar of unguent. Notice, too, Tobias' dog trailing at the angel's feet. Tobias is dressed, not in the manner of boys of Biblical times, but like a young Florentine of Lippi's own day. See how much more solid and better proportioned these figures are than those of Giotto, and how much better the artist understands the perspective of the background than does Castagno. A charming landscape of Lippi's own day stretches into the distance behind Tobias. But the lovely curling line of the billowing drapery is more like the delicate lines in Duccio's painting than it is like reality.

Sculptors, too, were busy with new discoveries. The first sculptors to imitate the works of Greece and Rome successfully were the Pisanos, father and son. These men worked in Pisa, a town near Florence, even before Giotto's day. Here we have a marble pulpit with the stories of *The Annunciation*, *The Nativity*, and *The Adoration of the Shepherds* in one framework by Niccolò Pisano (1220?–1278). The design of the whole scene is crowded and confusing and the sculptor has no idea of perspective. But the figures are more solid than any of the Gothic period, and the folds of their drapery deeper and more natural. In the two centuries following, sculptors studied every bone and muscle of the human body very carefully and by the time of Donatello (1386–1466), one of the greatest Renaissance sculptors, they understood perfectly how to represent the human body. The proportions of Donatello's *Saint George* are faultless, every muscle is in the right place, and we are sure he can move. He is a typical knight of fifteenth-century Florence, wide awake and ready to spring into action—very different from the quiet and peaceful figures in front of Gothic cathedrals.

The Annunciation, the Nativity, and the Adoration of the Shepherds, by Niccolò Pisano (1220?–1278)

58

Saint George, by Donatello (1386–1466)

The Adoration of the Magi, by Fra Angelico (1387–1455) and Fra Filippo Lippi (1406–1469)

We can get a most splendid idea of the brilliant, colorful, and sunny world of early Renaissance art from *The Adoration of the Magi,* a circular painting believed to be by two famous artists who were both monks, like the illuminators of medieval days —Fra (meaning Brother) Angelico (1387–1455), and Fra Filippo Lippi (1406–1469), who later left the orders, married, and became the father of Filippino Lippi. Here are the three Kings of the East who have been guided by the star of Bethlehem to the Christ Child, whom they have come to worship. How much color is to be seen in the great confusion of gesture and motion in the crowd of figures that disappear into the background! All is not perfect: we see the figures at a great distance a little too clearly; the hills in the background are not quite real, nor the perspective perfect; and the figures are still a bit medieval. But we are in a world of motion. This picture is particularly interesting because it is full of objects that "symbolize," or represent, thoughts and ideas that the painter wants us to understand. For example, the ruined building in the background is constructed in the style of the ancient Romans and represents the fall of paganism, the way of life of the unbelieving Romans before the coming of Christianity. The five little figures on the ruined wall may represent the athletes of virtue spoken of in the Bible when Saint Paul says, "Let us lay aside every weight . . . and let us run with patience the race that is set before us." And so almost every object and figure has its special meaning. Notice the little camels on the upper right side. They look almost more like big dogs. This is because the people of Italy were only just learning about the strange animals of the Orient, and did not have a very clear idea of what they looked like. The figures that fill this scene are dressed in the manner of the fifteenth century, and despite the camels the setting appears to be the Italy of the days of Angelico and Lippi.

As I have said, the people of the Renaissance were fond of portraits, such as this bust, or shoulder-length portrait, of Lorenzo de' Medici, said to be the work of the sculptor Verrocchio. No history of the Renaissance in Italy would be complete without mention of the Medici, the greatest family of the time. They were the true rulers of the city of Florence for three hundred years beginning in 1434, long after the struggle of the Guelphs and Ghibellines had ceased, although for much of that time they held no official title. Many people feel that the greatest member of this family was Lorenzo the Magnificent (1449–1492), whom we see here. He was so called because he was a great patron of the arts, who filled his palaces with masterpiece after masterpiece, and kept a brilliant court

Lorenzo de' Medici, by Verrocchio (1433–1488)

of learned men about him. Lorenzo was famous for his generosity and for his founding of many schools and universities. It is said that his dying words were that he regretted that he could not complete the libraries of his friends. Lorenzo was also a shrewd and stern ruler, and we may sense this when we look at Verrocchio's very real and unflattering portrait. He is truly a proud man of the Renaissance. Andrea del Verrocchio (1435–1488) was as famous a painter as he was a sculptor, and in his workshop there studied perhaps the greatest painter of all time, Leonardo da Vinci.

Giuliano de' Medici, by Botticelli (1444–1510)

Lorenzo the Magnificent had a younger brother called Giuliano who was known for his kindness and good nature. One day when they were both young men, while attending a service in Florence Cathedral, the two brothers were attacked by conspirators led by members of a rival family. Lorenzo himself escaped but Giuliano, who was unarmed, was stabbed to the heart. Here we see a portrait of the much-loved Giuliano by one of the greatest painters of the early Renaissance, Alessandro Botticelli (1444–1510). Botticelli must have been a short and tubby man, for his name means "little barrel." He was famous for his delightful pictures of a sunny and airy world, and in his painting we see a young man of light and gentle nature, but not without a resemblance to the sterner features of his brother Lorenzo. In the corner is painted a turtledove on a branch, and this again is "symbolism," for the dove represents mourning, either for Giuliano, or Giuliano's own grief for his beloved, Simonetta Vespucci, who died two years before he did.

With all the advances of the early Renaissance in Florence I have already mentioned, there was yet one more painter whose work led finally to the greatest age in the history of art. This was the man known as Masaccio (1401–1428). He must not have been a very pretty sight, this extraordinary painter, for his name means "Nasty Tom," and he died at the age of only twenty-seven, possibly in a street brawl. But however wild his private life may have been, Masaccio was a great artist. He portrayed his figures as strong and solid with heavy, realistic drapery. With him, there were no graceful, fluttery lines that were not true to life. He understood anatomy and perspective perfectly. See, for example, his *The Tribute Money*. Christ is telling His disciples to give unto Caesar what is Caesar's and unto God what is God's. The forms are solid and real—not like the graceful, weightless figures of Lippi or Fra Angelico. Masaccio bathed them in deep shadows, so that we can sense the air around them. The technique of painting and sculpture were now perfected, and the next period we are going to look at was perhaps the greatest in the history of art. It is known as the "High Renaissance."

The Tribute Money, by Masaccio (1401–1428)

XI

The High Renaissance

Now I am going to tell you about the three greatest artists of the greatest period in the history of art—the sixteenth century in Italy. Because the Renaissance, or rebirth, I spoke of in the last chapter reached its height at this time, this period is called the "High Renaissance."

The first of these artists is Leonardo da Vinci (1452–1519). Leonardo was born in the little town of Vinci, near Florence, the son of a successful lawyer. He showed great talent as an artist when he was still very young, and at the age of thirteen he became the apprentice of that same Verrocchio whose portrait bust of Lorenzo de' Medici we have seen. He remained with his master until the age of twenty-five, when he set up his own shop. By this time he was famous, not only as a painter, but as a man of science.

As a scientist, Leonardo was an extraordinary genius. He did not base his thinking on that of earlier scientists, but looked closely at everything in nature and described what he saw in great detail, with hundreds of beautiful and fascinating drawings. He filled up many notebooks with his observations of the world around him. For some reason that we do not know, he wrote these notes backwards, so that they could be read only when reflected in a mirror. He helped to found the sciences of geology (the study of the earth's surface) and botany (the study of plants), and he was a great engineer. He contributed much to the study of the human body, and was an expert at mathematics. He even studied the flight of birds, and tried to design an airplane driven by a propellor. See, for example, his plan for the building of a mechanical wing. He became famous as an inventor of all kinds of machines, and the princes of the age sought his aid in building weapons of war. Here is part of a letter he wrote to the Duke of Milan, a member of the great family of Sforza: "I have a method of constructing very light and portable bridges. . . . For the service of sieges, I am prepared to remove the water from ditches, and to make an infinite variety of scaling-ladders and other engines. . . . I have also most conven-

The Mona Lisa, by Leonardo da Vinci (1452–1519)

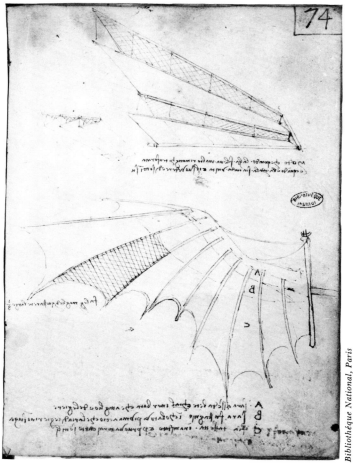

Page from a Notebook of
Leonardo da Vinci (1452–1519)

thinking about something, and we wonder what it is. Why is it that this picture seems to be more real than anything we have seen before? It is because the figure seems half hidden in deep shadows, and we cannot quite see its outlines. Isn't this the way we see things around us? We see the shape of a form and not its hard outline. Leonardo was the first painter who was able to show forms in this way, and now we really do see the misty air around the charming lady, and between her and the graceful view of hills and waters in the distance behind her.

Although he has left us few paintings, we have many of Leonardo's drawings, and so superb an artist was he that even these have the depth and beauty of great paintings. See, for example, his sketch of the head of a woman. Have you ever seen a more beautiful, more quiet, or more peaceful face? Is it surprising that many, perhaps most, people feel that Leonardo was the greatest artist that ever lived?

ient portable bombs. . . . I can construct covered wagons, secure and indestructible, which, entering in among the enemy, will break the strongest, and behind these the infantry can follow in safety. . . ." Yes, Leonardo invented the tank, and he was also one of the first men since the days of Greece and Rome to say that the sun stood still and did not move around the earth.

Although he was one of the greatest scientists of his time, it is as the greatest painter of his age that we think of Leonardo. He made art a kind of science, by studying the way in which the eye sees things, and he filled his notebooks with sketches of everything from the expression on the face of an angry man to the running water of a river. Unfortunately, Leonardo undertook very few works, and several of these he left unfinished. His most famous painting is the *Mona Lisa*, a portrait of a beautiful Florentine lady, and here we can see what a truly great painter Leonardo was. How perfectly he has shown the expression on the lady's face. She seems to be smiling at us, and yet she is

Drawing of the Head of a Woman,
by Leonardo da Vinci (1452–1519)

The Small Cowper Madonna, by Raphael (1483–1520)

Next I want to tell you about Raphael Santi, called simply Raphael (1483-1520). He was thirty-one years younger than Leonardo, and when he came to Florence from his native town of Urbino, Leonardo was considered the greatest painter of the day. The young Raphael soon became known, however, and because he was agreeable and sweet-natured, he was a favorite. He was asked to execute many altarpieces, frescoes, and portraits, and he had a large workshop with many assistants and apprentices to help him.

In Raphael's painting of Mary and the Christ Child, named *The Small Cowper Madonna* after an early owner, we can see that he followed Leonardo in showing his figures as heavy, rounded forms with deep shadows. And what a quiet, sunny scene this is. It is a good example of an excellent "composition." When we say that the "composition" of a picture is good, we mean that the figures and objects are so placed within the frame of the picture that the result is pleasing. Here the Madonna and the Christ Child whom she is gracefully holding form a triangle, with the Madonna's gentle face at the top.

Raphael was famous for the beauty of the people he painted. One day he wrote in a letter to Baldassare Castiglione, the greatest courtier of his time, of how he painted his beautiful figures. He said that he had no one model for any one figure, but he had many models in his mind, and tried to take the best from each. He did not try to copy nature, but like the Greeks I have told you about, he "idealized" it.

It is not surprising, then, that in his painting of the legend of Saint George and the Dragon, Saint George is seen as a handsome knight saving a beautiful fair-haired maiden. (You will remember that we have already seen a medieval statue of the same group.) Saint George is the patron saint of England, and so when a duke with the splendid name of Guidobaldo da Montefeltro of Urbino wanted to send a gift to King Henry VII of England, he commissioned Raphael to paint this subject. If you look closely at the picture, you will notice that Saint George is wearing the Order of the Garter—an honorary blue ribbon around his leg. It is to commemorate Henry's bestowal of this honor on Duke Guidobaldo himself. Notice, too, that the artist has signed the picture by writing "Raphello," one form of his name, on the horse's harness. It is small wonder that when Raphael died at the youthful age of thirty-seven he was mourned by all of Italy.

The third of these great artists was Michelangelo Buonarroti (1475-1564). He was the son of a noble family that had come upon bad days, and his father was very angry when he insisted that he wanted to become an artist. In the end, however, he gave his consent, and at the age of thirteen, young Michelangelo became the apprentice of a successful painter. At this time, as we have seen, Florence was ruled by the family of the Medici, who were crafty statesmen and great patrons of art. Lorenzo the Magnificent asked Michelangelo's master to send two of his brightest pupils to study the Greek and Roman statuary he had assembled in his gardens. Michelangelo was one of the students chosen, and from that day forward his greatest interest was in sculpture. It is said that once Lorenzo was walking through his gardens when he saw a young sculptor working on a head of a faun, a Greek nature god usually shown as a man with the legs of a goat. Lorenzo stopped and said to the boy jokingly, "Why, you have made this faun very old and yet you have left him all his teeth. Do you not know that men of that age always lack a few teeth?" When he came back the next day, he discovered that the young Michelangelo had removed a tooth from the head of the statue! So impressed was Lorenzo with the excellence of the boy's work that he invited him to live in his palace and treated him as a son.

By the time Michelangelo reached his early twenties, he was the most renowned sculptor in Italy. He did not open a shop like other sculptors, and he would not allow assistants to touch his work. Rather, he traveled around Italy working on the statues and paintings for which his patrons asked. In fact, his services were so in demand that the Pope threatened to declare war on the city of Florence if the Florentines did not send Michel-

Saint George and the Dragon, by Raphael (1483–1520)

angelo to him immediately. For once in history two powers almost came to blows over an artist!

There had lain for a hundred years in the stone-yards outside Florence a piece of marble that was so long and thin that no sculptor dared try to cut a figure from it. Michelangelo, however, took up the challenge. For two years he labored on the block in secret, but when he finally showed his work to the citizens of Florence, they were astonished, for it was one of the greatest statues ever made. The sculptor had turned this difficult block of marble into his famous statue of *David*, the Biblical hero who, as a boy, slew the giant Goliath with his sling. How strong and noble, full of life and strength, this young boy is. Michelangelo was as great a student of anatomy as was Leonardo, and here we see every vein, every muscle, and every nerve of an alert young man. He seems to challenge the world. This great strength and force can be seen in much of Michelangelo's work.

See, too, his figure of Giuliano de' Medici from the tomb Michelangelo decorated for him in the

David, by Michelangelo (1475–1564)

Giuliano de' Medici, by Michelangelo (1475–1564)

Medici Chapel in Florence. This is not actually a portrait of Giuliano, nephew of the unfortunate young man whose sad fate we have already seen, but an idealized figure of a man of action, about to spring up. Have you ever seen such life and energy in a marble figure? How quiet the Greek statues seem by comparison.

And yet not all Michelangelo's works are famous for motion and life. His *Pietà*, or figure of Mary grieving over the body of Christ, is one of the most calmly beautiful statues ever made. The body of Christ is limp, and Mary grieves silently—her only expression is one of peace. See, too, the *Bound Slave*. His head falls back in exhaustion, and although he strains every muscle, he cannot move. But who is the slave? And by what power is he held in servitude? Perhaps he is meant to represent mankind's struggle against the forces of evil. Michelangelo does not tell us, and that is the strength and mystery of the work.

Some of his finest work, however, was not in sculpture but in painting. The Pope wanted the

Pietà, by Michelangelo (1475–1564)

ceiling of the Sistine Chapel in Rome covered with frescoes. He asked Michelangelo to paint them, but the master said that he was a sculptor and not a painter. The Pope insisted, however, and eventually Michelangelo agreed to the task, although it was a very difficult one. For four years he lay on his back on a scaffold sixty feet above the ground, and painted on a surface above his head.

Bound Slave, by Michelangelo (1475–1564)

Giraudon

Anderson

The Delphic Sibyl, by Michelangelo (1475–1564)

All the same, when he was finished, his decorations were among the greatest works of art of all time. He covered the huge ceiling with scenes from the history of mankind as told in the Old Testament, such as the story of the Creation and the Garden of Eden. Never have figures been painted with such strength and force. We see, too, all the Prophets of the Old Testament, and also those who foretold the future to the Greeks and Romans—the "oracles" or Sibyls. Look at the famous *Delphic Sibyl.* How grand is her gesture as she looks up from her scroll and foretells the future. Although the figure is twisted, every line of anatomy is perfect. Still, we cannot forget that Michelangelo was first of all a sculptor, for his figures seem almost like marvelous sculpture in relief on the ceiling itself.

XII

Magnificent Venice

In northern Italy, on the shore of the Adriatic Sea, lies one of the most romantic cities in history— Venice. Florence was not the only center for artists in the period we call the High Renaissance. Venice had her masters too.

You have all seen pictures of Venice, the fabulous city of spires and colored marble palaces, where streets are canals and the people travel in long graceful boats called gondolas, guided through the water by gondoliers who ply long barge poles. In the days of the Renaissance, Venice was at her height. Most of her citizens were wealthy merchants, and at times even pirates, who brought the luxuries of China and India to their city, the most important port on the east coast of Italy, and there sold them to the traders of the towns further inland. The money they gained they spent on display. Nothing in Italy could equal the magnificent private palaces and churches that were reflected in the waters of Venice. What is more, Venice was a peaceful city. There was none of the violence we found in Florence. The government

was left to a council of nobles and their head, called the Doge. They did not strive among themselves for power, and if there was any chance of an attack from an enemy, they hired foreign soldiers to fight their battles for them.

Above all, the people of Venice loved gaiety and a carefree life of pleasure. They had many public pageants in which the officials wore the most costly and magnificent dress, and every year they celebrated their famous carnival, with masked balls and every kind of entertainment. They devoted little time to serious thought, and so they had only a few great writers, but they did love beauty and they encouraged painters, heaping every honor on them.

Venetian painters were the first to use oil paint in the way it has been used ever since. Oil painting was said to have begun in the North, as I will explain to you in the next chapter, but the Venetians were the first to use layer after layer of rich oil paint on a piece of stretched canvas rather than a wooden board. Above all, the Venetians

73

The Adoration of the Shepherds, by Giorgione (1478–1510)

were famous for the richness of the brilliant colors in their paintings, as we shall see in some of the pictures at which we are going to look.

Many feel that the greatness of Venetian painting started with Giorgione (1477–1510). We know very little of his life, except that he lived to be only thirty-three, and left very few pictures behind. But how great these are! It is said that Giorgione was the first to use the beautiful soft light and rich color that made Venetian painting famous. He worked at about the same time as Leonardo and Raphael, and in his work, too, we see rounded forms in deep shadows. Indeed, if he had lived longer he might well have been as famous as were they. Giorgione particularly liked country scenes with a few quiet figures, and his *Adoration of the Shepherds* is such a painting. The shepherds who came to worship the Christ Child were a subject often painted in the Renaissance, as we have seen, and it was rarely more beautifully done than by Giorgione.

The most successful of all the Venetian painters was Titian (1477–1576). He was born in the Alps near Venice around the same time as Giorgione, and the story goes that when he was a little boy he painted a picture of a Madonna using the juices of different flowers for paint, and that it was so excellent that he was sent to study with a master in Venice. Whether this story is true or not, Titian was a brilliant pupil and later in life became one of the most famous painters of the sixteenth century. He lived to the age of ninety-nine and painted almost until his last day. During his long life Titian was greatly honored. He painted popes and kings, and the Emperor Charles V, who then ruled most of Europe, bestowed on him the title of Count Palatine. It is said that the Emperor once actually bent down to pick up Titian's brush for him, and according to another story, the Emperor bade Titian to ride by his side, saying, "I can make as many lords as I wish, but only God can make a Titian."

The Venetians loved to cover the walls of their palaces with paintings of themselves in all their finery, and Titian was a particularly great portrait painter. In his painting of Ranuccio Farnese, we see a young boy of the Renaissance. At the time this picture was painted, Ranuccio, who was perhaps fourteen years old, was a student of Classical languages at Padua, and already the prior of a monastery—the very youngest members of noble families were showered with honors. And yet Ranuccio, for all his proud stance and rich dress, looks very like any boy one might see today—Titian has captured the soft look of the young boy as well as he has painted the fine texture of his silk doublet and coat. He, too, like Leonardo da Vinci and Giorgione, often put his figures in deep shadow.

Titian painted many works during his long life much in the style of the other painters of Venice. In his old age, however, he began to lose his sight, and to paint in a most unusual way. He would paint a figure with just a few strokes of the brush, instead of representing every detail carefully. This way of showing an object, which gives us the "impression" that the figure is before us although we do not see it in every detail, was to become much more important in the following centuries, and for this reason Titian is called "the father of modern painting."

Titian had a studio with many apprentices, and the most talented of these was Tintoretto (1518–1594). There is a story that, when he saw some sketches that the young Tintoretto had made, Titian ordered him to leave his studio—whether from jealousy, or because he felt the young man had no more to learn, we do not know. In any case, Tintoretto was a most exciting painter. Let us look at his picture of *The Conversion of Saint Paul*. In the midst of battle Paul is said to have had a vision of heavenly light that threw him to the ground and terrified the soldiers with him. Have we ever seen such tremendous motion and excitement in a painting before? We see figures in every position—how well the lessons of Castagno and the other students of anatomy had been learned! And how far into the distance the action continues! There is no "foreground" and "background"; it is all one scene. It was at this time that huge and decorative paintings full of color and fluttering motion became very much the style,

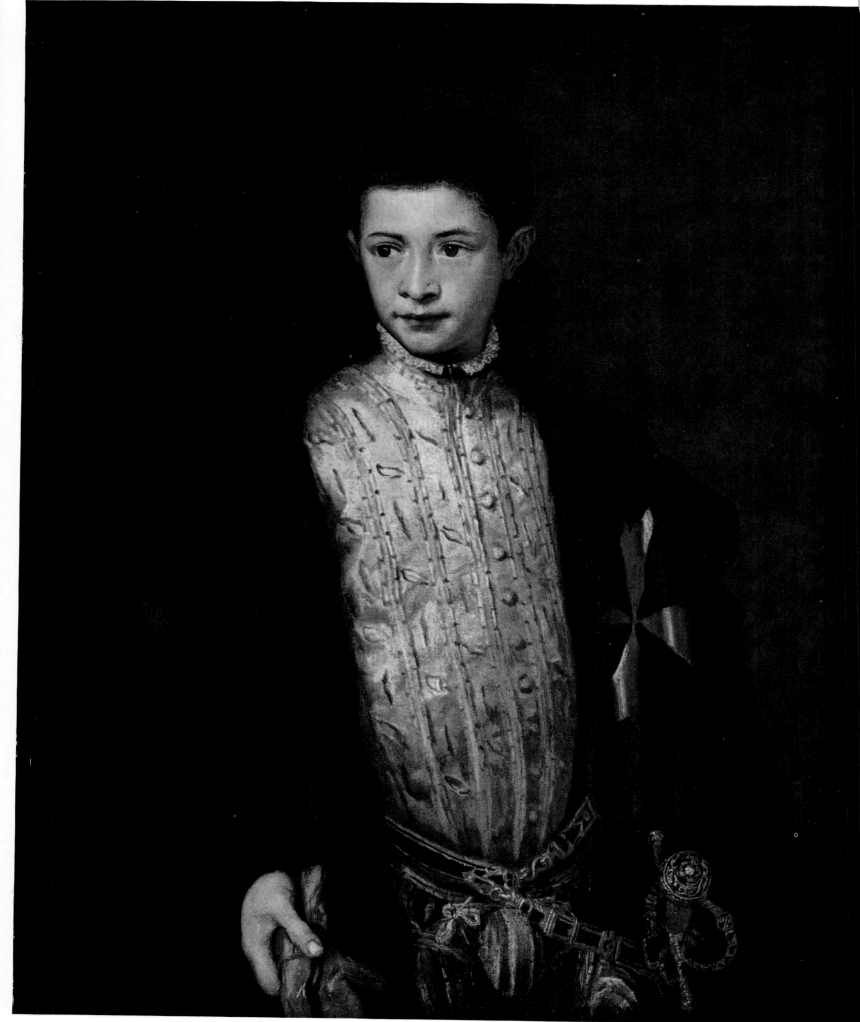

Ranuccio Farnese, by Titian (1477–1576)

The Conversion of Saint Paul, by Tintoretto (1518–1594)

and this is known as the "Baroque" period.

Whether the Venetians painted scenes from the Bible, history, or mythology, they were often really painting the nobles of Venice and their ladies. See *The Finding of Moses* by Paolo Veronese (1528–1588), who, like Tintoretto, painted huge colorful and decorative scenes. Here we see the finding of the infant Moses, the future leader of the Israelites, as he was floating in a basket in the bulrushes, by the daughter of the Pharaoh of Egypt and her attendants. Now all this took place in the time of the ancient Egyptians, but these are not dark Egyptian women wearing the dress of an early time, such as those whose pictures we have seen in the tombs along the Nile, but blond Venetian ladies dressed as Veronese must have seen them attending some ceremony on the Grand Canal in Venice, even accompanied, as Venetian ladies might be, by a dwarf in jester's costume!

This colorful and brilliant style was continued in Venice during the next two centuries, when the change we call "the Renaissance" had spread throughout Europe. Giovanni Battista Tiepolo (1696–1770), who lived a century after Tintoretto and Veronese, was famous, too, for his huge and decorative murals. We can get some idea of what his style was like from his drawing of *Two Magicians and a Youth*. The Venetians loved tales of

View Through an Archway, by Guardi (1712–1793)

magic and sorcery, and the subject might be a frightening one, with two sinister old men standing over a young boy, but Tiepolo's line is so light and decorative we cannot take the matter very seriously.

Venice was one of the most beautiful cities in the world, and people elsewhere loved to see scenes of its canals and streets. In the eighteenth century, when Tiepolo was painting, there were two artists who became very famous for their beautiful scenes of Venice. These were Canaletto (1697–1768) and Guardi (1712–1793). When we look at Canaletto's *View in Venice* we can get some idea of what a really beautiful city it was, with its lovely statues, proud buildings, and peaceful canals. We can well imagine the gondola we see here, carrying some beautiful lady to meet a handsome nobleman who will come whirling down the steps in a black cape, doffing his three-cornered hat to greet her. Or let us peer into Guardi's *View Through an Archway* —what business might be discussed, or what plots hatched, in the shadows of such a courtyard!

Two Magicians and a Youth, by Tiepolo (1696–1770)

The Finding of Moses, by Veronese (1528–1588)

View in Venice, by Canaletto (1697–1768)

XIII

The Renaissance Comes to the North

Thus far we have been speaking of the artists of Italy alone, but their new discoveries soon spread across the Alps to the Netherlands, then called "Flanders," and Germany. Here too, cities were growing rich with new trade from the East and the development of their own industries, such as the weaving of cloth. This does not sound so very different from what was happening in Italy. But in the North the cities grew, not around the courts of one or two very wealthy merchant princes, but around large groups of merchants who were prosperous, although not "princely" in their wealth. They appreciated fine painting, as we shall see, but only in the way that business men do today, as a decoration for their homes and as an occasional interest. There were no great patrons who supported schools of art, and the painter was still a tradesman as he had been in Gothic times, and not a public figure entertained by kings and followed by crowds.

The first true painters of the Renaissance in the North were the Van Eyck brothers. The painting of *The Annunciation* by Jan van Eyck (1380?–1441) is ample proof that the Flemish artists could, if they chose, equal those of Italy. The Annunciation, as we have seen, is the moment at which the Angel Gabriel comes to Mary and tells her she will become the mother of Christ. This painting was meant to be part of an altarpiece that was never finished. It was painted at the time Masaccio was experimenting in Italy, and it would seem that the artist has already solved many of the problems of the Renaissance. His figures are a bit stiff, and do not show the vigorous, free motion of those of Masaccio—in fact, they look very like the fragile figures we have already seen in Gothic churches, with their long, delicate hands and faces. But if you look closely you will see that this picture is very different from the flat painting by Duccio of *The Calling of the Apostles Peter and Andrew*. Notice with what almost perfect perspective the room has been drawn, how well the artist has captured the effect of the dim, shadowy light and air within the enclosed space of a church,

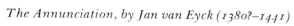

The Annunciation, by Jan van Eyck (1380?–1441)

and how naturally the light seems to come through the window. We feel we could almost step into the church ourselves. This is because the artist, like his fellows in Italy, has been studying nature as he sees it with his own eyes. But while the painters of Italy made a special study of the anatomy of the body, and of how to show movement, the painters of the North specialized in studying the surface of everything they painted—its texture, its color, and the effect light had upon it— and they carefully put upon the canvas every tiny detail that caught their eye. See, for example, how perfectly the stiff brocade of the angel's cloak and the soft brocade of the pillow on the stool in the foreground have been painted, and how perfectly the wood of the stool itself imitates reality. The painting is full of details—notice that the floor is covered with tiny scenes from the Old Testament. Surely, the painter has not much to learn.

The most important revolution in the technique of painting is also attributed to the Van Eycks. It is said that they were the first to mix powdered color with oil, instead of with egg as had formerly been done, thus inventing the slow-drying oil paint used by all the great masters since the Renaissance. And so there were things that Italy had to learn from the North, too.

For some strange reason, the Van Eycks had no followers. The other painters of the fifteenth century in the North continued in the Gothic style. It was not until the next century that further strides were made, and then in Germany.

At the end of the fifteenth century there was born the greatest German artist, Albrecht Dürer (1471–1528). He was a "contemporary" of, which is to say he lived at the same time as, Michelangelo, Raphael, and Leonardo da Vinci in Italy. As a boy he was apprenticed first to a painter and woodblock maker and then to an engraver. I must mention here that a century earlier a method of reproducing a picture many times over had been discovered. This was the "woodblock." The artist merely cut away the surface of the block except for the lines he wanted to reproduce and then covered the block with ink and pressed it on successive pieces of paper. Shortly after, this method

was improved by the use of a copper plate. The artist would cut the lines he wanted into the plate and then fill them with ink—the reverse of what is done in the woodblock—and press this plate onto paper, making a more detailed picture. This system was called "engraving," and both woodcuts and engravings became very popular in the North, and were widely used to illustrate the Bible. When young Dürer had become an expert woodcutter and engraver, he went to Italy to study painting, and came back determined to bring to the artists of his own country, not only all the lessons that the Van Eycks had already learned, but also a splendid knowledge of anatomy and the ability to give complete freedom of motion to their figures. He made many scientific studies of anatomy, and was in this way somewhat like Leonardo. But the Germans of Dürer's day were still far more like the men of the Middle Ages than were the people of Italy. They believed more strongly in the Bible and had less knowledge of the world and of Greek

Saint Eustace, by Dürer (1471–1528)

Saint Burchard of Würzburg, by Tilman Riemenschneider (1460?–1531)

and Roman writings, and Dürer made pictures to suit their tastes and beliefs. See, for example, his engraving of Saint Eustace, when Christ appeared to him in the form of a stag he was about to kill. It is a religious picture, but it is set in the world of Dürer's time in Germany—which was still the medieval world of the fairy tales of the Brothers Grimm. Indeed, this might be a hunting scene from a fairy tale, with an enchanted castle in the background, swans on a lake, a rider in medieval dress, with his horse and dogs—but still it is a picture of the Renaissance. See how, as in the works of the Van Eycks, every detail of the surfaces is perfect, even though this is an engraving and not a painting. Every hair on the dog's back, every blade of grass is as it should be. Dürer has noticed everything, even the swarm of birds around the castle tower. But most important of all, Dürer understands anatomy as well as any painter of the South. His dogs might spring up, Saint Eustace might leap on his horse and gallop off—every muscle is perfect.

The North had its sculptors, too. See the head of a German saint by Tilman Riemenschneider (1460?–1531), who lived at the same time as Dürer. Again, it looks as if the Gothic style has lingered on. The figure with its flat folded drapery and long hands looks more like a statue from a Gothic church than like the active *Saint George* of Donatello, or Michelangelo's *David*. But look at the face. It isn't "idealized," simple, and beautiful, as Gothic faces usually are; it is a portrait of a real man, tired and full of sadness. We could well believe him to be a saint.

During this time, a movement known as the "Reformation" was taking place. Led by the cleric Martin Luther, the people of the northern countries strongly criticized the luxurious life of the clergy of the Catholic Church in Rome. Germany and then the northern Netherlands broke away and established their own churches, and later England followed suit. This was the founding of Protestantism. The new churches of the Protestant faith were to be very simple and to have no rich decorations to distract the mind from thoughts of God and what was truly good. And so it followed that there were fewer important paintings commissioned for churches. As it happened, the next great painter in Germany, Hans Holbein (1497–1543), was famous for his portraits, and these are among the finest ever painted. By now the artists of the North had learned all that Italy had to offer, and Holbein's portraits were perfect likenesses of his subjects; if a subject's character was reflected in his face, then Holbein reproduced that character exactly in his portrait. But if he had learned the mastery of the human body from the Italians, he had learned how to portray perfectly the surfaces of things—the texture of skin and cloth and fur—from the Van Eycks.

Holbein settled originally in Switzerland, but later moved to England, where he became court painter to Henry VIII. We all know many stories of Henry and how "six wives he wedded, one died, one survived, two divorced and two beheaded," and how he drove the Catholic Church out of England. Thanks to Holbein we know exactly how many of the actors in this strange performance

Edward VI as a Child, by Holbein (1497–1543)

PARVVLE PATRISSA, PATRIÆ VIRTVTIS ET HÆRES
ESTO, NIHIL MAIVS MAXIMVS ORBIS HABET.
GNATVM VIX POSSVNT COELVM ET NATVRA DEDISSE,
HVIVS QVEM PATRIS, VICTVS HONORET HONOS.
ÆQVATO TANTVM, TANTI TV FACTA PARENTIS,
VOTA HOMINVM, VIX QVO PROGRFDIANTVR, HABENT
VINCITO, VICISTI. QVOT REGES PRISCVS ADORAT
ORBIS, NEC TE QVI VINCERE POSSIT, ERIT.
Ricard Morysing Car

appeared, for he painted all the great men and women of Henry's reign in every detail and without one line of flattery. In fact, it is said that Henry agreed to marry one of his wives on the strength of Holbein's portrait of her. Here is his portrait of Henry's son and heir, Edward VI, as a tiny child. It was given to the King on New Year's Day, 1539, and the inscription beneath the portrait reads, "Little one, emulate thy father: Be heir to the virtue of him whose equal the world does not possess. Heaven and Earth could hardly produce a son to surpass in glory such a father. Do but match in full thy parent's deeds, and men can ask no more. Shouldst thou surpass him, thou hast outstript all kings the world revered in ages past." You may think no child ever looked so solemn, or ever made such a regal gesture with one hand while he grasped a baby's rattle with the other, but I suppose we can forgive Holbein for flattering such a tiny subject. Alas, Edward VI died at the age of sixteen, and never lived up to such grand expectations as these—that was left to his older sister, who became Queen Elizabeth I.

There were no great painters in Germany after Holbein, and from the end of the sixteenth century onward the talent for painting seemed to have returned to the Netherlands, and particularly to Holland, as that part of Flanders which had become Protestant was now called. As you remember, no great religious pictures were now commissioned, and as there were no wealthy princes who owned huge palaces, there was no opportunity for the painting of large murals on mythological and heroic subjects, nor was there any place for statuary, except the town squares, and so there were no great sculptors. The townsmen, or "burghers," of Holland wanted small paintings to hang in their modest homes. What they liked to see were pictures of the familiar world around them: the interior of their homes, family gatherings, peasants at work or play, the quiet Dutch countryside, or the sea that beat on its shores. They did not care for the imaginative scenes from the Bible or Greek and Latin mythology of which the merchants of Venice were so fond; they wanted only portraits of themselves and their families and pic-

tures of what they could immediately recognize, and at these the Dutch painters excelled. The painting by Pieter de Hooch (1629?–1683) of a Dutch courtyard was exactly to their taste. Here we see a simple scene of a family having a quiet drink around a table in their back yard. As ever with the painters of the North, the surface of things is very perfectly done. What could look more real to the touch than the bricks on the wall or the uneven floor of the courtyard? The Dutch liked to see all the members of a family in their pictures, including the children.

They liked scenes of action and family "situations" as well. Such a painting is *The Suitor's Visit* by Gerard ter Borch (1617–1681). A young man has come to pay his respects to a young lady, and he makes a sweeping bow as he enters. The young lady is shy and blushes, but she looks pleased—a very different sort of scene from anything that would have appealed to the merchants of Venice. But still, they would have admired the way the painter has caught the richness of the young lady's white satin skirt!

Frans Hals (1580–1666), another master of the seventeenth century in Holland, is famous for his casual and unposed portraits showing the fat, pink-cheeked, and jolly burghers as they must surely have looked—and how different they appear to be from the stately Italians of a century before! Or is it just that the Italian artist has posed his model, and the Dutch painter has deliberately caught his at an odd moment? The officer in Hals's portrait looks as if he is about to burst out laughing, and his eyes are full of amusement and life. We do not know exactly who the subject of this portrait is, but he was an officer of some sort, and, as we can see the sea through the window behind him, the artist may be telling us that he is a naval officer.

Probably the greatest painter of everyday Dutch life was Jan Vermeer van Delft (1632–1675), whose works are very rare. Vermeer painted quiet indoor scenes with one or two figures going about their daily chores—a woman kneading bread or sewing, or a painter at his easel. There is not much motion in these scenes, but never, before or since, has a painter achieved such a photographic like-

A Dutch Courtyard, by Pieter de Hooch (1629?–1683)

The Suitor's Visit, by Gerard ter Borch (1617–1681)

Portrait of an Officer, by Frans Hals (1580–1666)

Young Girl with a Flute, by Vermeer (1632–1675)

ness of reality. When it comes to transferring to canvas the surface texture of things and the effect of light and air, one would not have felt it was possible to surpass Van Eyck or Holbein, and yet

Vermeer has done so. In his picture entitled *Young Girl with a Flute,* the colors are dulled, as they appear to be in a darkened room in the fading light of late afternoon. Could you ever believe that

90

a figure seated near a window and dressed in heavy silk and fur could find its way so perfectly onto the flat surface of a painting? Isn't it perhaps even more true to nature than a photograph? The girl seems to be saying something, but this is far less important to the artist than the light that falls on her and the texture of her dress.

The first landscape, which is to say a country scene in which there are no human figures or the figures are of little importance, was painted by a German artist in the early sixteenth century. During the seventeenth century, however, the painting of landscapes and seascapes (a seascape is a painting of the sea, often with ships, but with few or no human figures) was perfected by Dutch artists, for they were a favorite kind of picture in the North. The Italian artists painted many very beautiful landscapes, but always as the background for some human figure. In the work of Dutch painters, such as the *Forest Scene* by Jacob

van Ruisdael (1628–1682), the setting alone is important, and clouds blown across the sky and trees lashed by the winds provide the only movement.

One other new type of picture came into being to please the tastes of the townsmen of Holland, and this is the "still life." A "still life" is a painting of a few household objects grouped together to form a graceful composition. There are no human figures and no motion; the object is to make each thing painted appear as real as possible, and this well suited the Dutch painter's talent for portraying surface texture. Let us look at a *Still Life* by Jan Davidsz de Heem (1606–1683). Here we see a chair and table loaded with lobster and all kinds of luscious fruit—grapes, peaches, peeled lemon, and such. On the table, too, are the most beautiful silver and glass, and cloths of the finest linen. Each object is so placed as to form the most varied and interesting composition, and painted so perfectly that one feels that one could touch it.

Still Life, by De Heem (1606–1683)

Forest Scene, by Jacob van Ruisdael (1628–1682)

XIV

The Masters of the North

There are two great painters of the North that we have not yet discussed, and they were the very greatest indeed. I am speaking of Peter Paul Rubens (1577–1640) and Rembrandt van Rijn (1606–1669), known simply as Rembrandt. They both came from the same kind of home and studied under the same kind of masters; but while they were in some ways very much alike, in other ways they were the very opposite of each other.

Peter Paul Rubens lived in the part of Flanders now called Belgium, after it had been separated from Holland, and so, unlike the Dutch painters we have seen, he was brought up in a Catholic country where painting for the Church was still very important, and where artists imitated the works of the Italian masters. Rubens was the son of a successful lawyer, and when he was a child he was a brilliant student, not of painting, but of Latin. In fact, as a young man he could speak seven languages with ease. When he was thirteen years old, his mother sent him to be a page at court, hoping to make of him a gentleman and a lawyer. But

after a year Peter Paul decided that he would not be a courtier, but rather an artist. Needless to say, his family did not approve, for the country was full of painters, and they were not very much admired. But young Rubens won out and became the apprentice of a local artist. And how well he succeeded! When he was twenty-three he traveled to Italy to study the works of Leonardo, Michelangelo, and Titian, but he was already such a fine artist himself that the Duke of Mantua invited him to become his court painter. Nor was he merely another artist. Rubens was an accomplished gentleman—tall, handsome, and beautifully dressed, with perfect manners and a knowledge of many languages. In fact, the Duke was so impressed that he sent the young man as his ambassador to the court of Philip III in Spain. Rubens was to bring with him many rich gifts from the Duke and, among them, several very valuable paintings. The story goes that when the boat arrived in Spain the paintings had been ruined by the dampness of the trip. Never daunted, Rubens restored those that could be saved, and quickly painted pictures of his own to replace those that were hopeless. The King and Queen were delighted with both Rubens and his paintings, and the trip was a great success.

Shortly after his return to Italy, Rubens heard that his mother was very ill, and so he left immediately for Flanders. Unfortunately, although he rode at top speed, he arrived too late to see his mother alive. Still, once home, he decided to settle down. It was a wise decision, for he was immediately a great success, and the Spanish viceroys who ruled Belgium invited him to become their court painter. He set up his studio in his native town of Antwerp, and what a studio! He bought a magnificent mansion and filled it with costly antiques and splendid statues and paintings by the masters of the Renaissance. Here he made a perfect home for the beautiful young wife he had just married. All the great men of his day flocked around him, philosophers and statesmen, and commissions flooded in from all sides—portraits, altarpieces, huge paintings to decorate the walls of churches and palaces. Rubens was often called upon, too, as a diplomat, to arrange agreements between the rulers of Europe. So successful was he that Philip IV of Spain presented him with a title of nobility and he was knighted by Charles I of England.

And what were his paintings like? They were huge decorations full of sunshine and life—they were "Baroque," like those of Tintoretto and Veronese. Rubens loved to paint large canvases with many healthy figures full of action and beautifully grouped. Whether he was painting a scene from the Bible or from ancient mythology, he filled his pictures with light and action. See, for example, his painting of *Decius Mus Addressing the Legions*. There is a story in the works of the Roman author Livy that when the Roman troops were besieging the city of Capua, their general, Decius Mus, was told in a dream that either the army or its leader must fall. He determined to give his own life, and he is seen here telling the sorry news to his commanders. This painting is in fact probably a sketch for a tapestry, and is not properly finished, but it gives us a good idea of Rubens' work. We can see how he loved to fill his pictures

with vigorous motion, rich decoration, and warm, brilliant colors—bright reds, blues, golds, and greens, and the color of flesh.

Rubens had a huge workshop with many assistants and apprentices who helped him with the hundreds of pictures he undertook to paint. Sometimes he would give his helpers a small sketch of a picture, and when they had painted it on a larger canvas, he would finish it with his own masterly brush strokes. Then too, certain artists in the workshop who were particularly good at one thing, such as animals or background scenery, would be called in to paint these parts of a picture. So not all paintings with Rubens' signature were done entirely by the master himself, and some people feel that Rubens' workshop was very like a picture factory. Still, there was nothing new about the idea of having assistants that painted parts of pictures, for many of the great masters of the Renaissance that we have seen signed pictures that were done in just this way. Do not forget that in those days, painting was still considered a trade. If a cabinet-maker could have a workshop of assistants, why couldn't a painter?

In fact, parts of some of Rubens' greatest paintings were done by his most successful pupil, Anthony Van Dyck (1599–1641). Van Dyck became the most famous portraitist of his day, and was invited to go to England as court painter to Charles I. He was not as great as his teacher, for his pictures lack life, but he painted many fine portraits that you may see hanging in the great houses of Europe today—pictures of distinguished men and women, splendidly dressed, for he was a great master of the texture of fine cloth. His portrait of Clelia Cattaneo, the daughter of an Italian marchesa, is a picture of an appealing little girl, for all the greatness of her family and the richness of her lace dress.

Rembrandt van Rijn started life very much as Rubens had, except for the fact that he was a generation younger and born in Protestant Holland. He was the son of a wealthy miller, and his family sent him to a Latin school in Leyden, hoping that he would become a doctor. But the young Rembrandt, like the young Rubens, had other ideas,

Decius Mus Addressing the Legions, by Rubens (1577–1640)

Clelia Cattaneo, Daughter of Marchesa Elena Grimaldi, by Van Dyck (1599–1641)

and turned to painting. Like Rubens, he was apprenticed with the local Dutch painters, and showed so much talent that he was soon on his own. He was already a successful artist in Leyden at twenty-one, and when he was twenty-six he moved to Amsterdam and was a still greater success. Here he, like Rubens, married a beautiful young girl and bought a fine house which he filled with handsome furniture and great works by other painters. He never thought about money, and loved to buy rich clothing and jewelry for his wife, who was herself an heiress.

As we have seen, the Dutch had no use for huge decorative scenes for churches and palaces such as Rubens painted, but they loved portraits of themselves, and Rembrandt was considered the best portraitist in Amsterdam. Nobody could paint the texture of skin, cloth, and fur as he could, or capture so perfect a likeness, not only of a person's face, but of the very character behind it.

But as time went on, there came a change in Rembrandt's work. He had a great sense of the unhappiness of men. He did not always want to paint the handsome, rich burghers of Amsterdam; he found beauty in the faces of old people and of those who had suffered. He wanted to paint pictures full of shadows that made one feel the mystery and sadness of life. These things were not popular with the tradesmen who bought his paintings, and Rembrandt wanted to please them so that he could afford a fine home for his wife. But three of his four children had died, and when his wife became very ill, he began not to care. Sixteen members of the "civic guard," or citizen army, asked him to paint a group portrait to hang in the Hall of the Musketeers. The painting, called *The Night Watch*, caused an uproar. The sixteen burghers had expected to see clear portraits of themselves in a group. But instead—what a dramatic scene! The guard has just been called to

The Night Watch, by Rembrandt (1606–1669)

arms, and Rembrandt has painted them stumbling around in confusion in the darkness. Only two members, the Captain and Lieutenant, are in a strong light. The picture is full of suspense and excitement, but only two of the sixteen men who had paid for the portrait could recognize themselves! After the scandal of *The Night Watch,* Rembrandt had few commissions for portraits, and finally none, but it didn't matter; his wife had died, and he no longer cared for money or what it could buy. He now turned to painting the sadness of life as it had never been painted before, and it is most deeply to be seen in his own face as he put it on canvas in his old age. Rembrandt did several portraits of himself, and they are among the most moving pictures ever painted. How much wisdom do we see if we look into those dark eyes, and how much suffering—not only the artist's own, but that of all men.

Rembrandt did not work in paint alone. He also loved to make etchings (an etching is a kind of engraving), and these are very beautiful compo-sitions in black and white, as Rembrandt was the greatest etcher that ever lived. He loved the Bible and did many etchings of scenes from it, not for churches, and not for buyers, as Biblical scenes were unpopular in Holland, but for himself. His figures are not idealized like those of the Renais-sance painters, perfect in beauty and grace. See, for example, his *Christ with the Sick Around Him.* Rembrandt found his models on the streets in the poor sections of Amsterdam, and they are real people, although strangely dressed in the robes of Easterners that he had seen in the busy port, or as he imagined they would look. They are dim figures whom we can just glimpse in the shadows, and on their faces we can see the unhappiness of a lifetime.

When he died, a penniless old man, Rembrandt had already buried his only surviving son. Yet he could not have felt that his life was wasted, for he had painted some of the greatest works in the history of art. It is certain that as Rubens was the painter of happiness and the joy of life, Rembrandt was the painter of life's grief.

Christ with the Sick Around Him, by Rembrandt (1606–1669)

Self-Portrait, by Rembrandt (1606–1669)

XV

Art in Spain

In 1492, the very year Columbus discovered America, King Ferdinand and Queen Isabella won the last battle in a long war to drive the Moors out of Spain, and established a strong Catholic rule. The Moors were followers of the Mohammedan faith who had invaded Spain from North Africa in the eighth century, and had brought the culture of the East with them. It was against their religion to portray the human form, and so they left behind no important paintings and sculpture, but they did love to decorate their palaces and mosques (their places of worship) with beautiful and intricate floral designs in both carvings and mosaics, and their richly ornamented buildings are to be found throughout North Africa and in Spain as well, where the Alhambra in Granada is considered one of the most beautiful palaces in the world.

With the coming of Ferdinand and Isabella there was a strong central monarchy in Spain; there were no city-states, as in Italy, or important towns as in Germany and the Netherlands, with many merchants and tradesmen. In Spain, and in

France, as we shall see in the next chapter, everything revolved around the court of the king, and artists who followed in the Italian tradition painted portraits of the kings and nobles of their court. There were religious paintings, too, to decorate churches—of which there were many indeed in Spain, for the Spanish were deeply attached to the Catholic faith. They took their religion very seriously, more seriously than the people of any other country in Europe, for they felt it was necessary to destroy every trace of the influence of the Moors.

The great Spanish painters leave us with a clear picture of what their court was like. It was certainly very rich, for the gold and silver of the mines of newly discovered South America were pouring into the coffers of the king. But the Spaniards were of a somber and doleful character, and this too can be seen in their paintings, and especially in the strange work of Spain's first great painter, El Greco (1541-1614), who lived during the second half of the sixteenth century, at the time when Tintoretto was painting in Venice. El Greco was

100

Saint Martin and the Beggar, by El Greco (1541–1614)

Portrait of a Young Man, by Velásquez (1599–1660)

not in fact a Spaniard, but a Greek, and the name by which he is known simply means "The Greek" in Spanish. On his way from Greece to Spain, El Greco studied painting in Venice, but his work is very different from the colorful Italian masterpieces, perhaps because of the mournful influences of the Spanish court. Let us look at his painting of *Saint Martin and the Beggar.* Saint Martin, seen as a soldier, is in the act of cutting his cloak in two so that he can give half of it to a naked beggar.

El Greco's colors are such as had never been seen before in painting—they have been said to be like the "colors of the moon"—pale and steely grays, purples, bright blues, and lemon greens, and his pictures often appear rather frightening, as if seen in the light of an oncoming storm. What is more, he often painted his figures, as he has here, to make them appear longer than would be natural, and more twisted. He did so in order to gain the most dramatic and impressive effect, particularly when, as here, the painting had a religious meaning. This is called "distortion." In former times artists who were unable to draw correctly "distorted" their figures by mistake, but El Greco was the first to do so deliberately, and, as we shall see later, this was of great importance.

In the years after his death, El Greco was considered to have been a poor painter because of his distortion of figures, but he was successful during his lifetime, and the nobles of the court flocked to his studio. If you go to Toledo in Spain today, you can see the house in which he lived, exactly as it was then, even to the tiny chairs he had made for the room in which his children played—for, despite the odd character of his paintings, El Greco is known to have been a kind and amiable man.

In the next generation, the greatest painter in Spain was Diego Velásquez (1599–1660), who was court painter to King Philip IV. Velásquez's work was far less unusual than that of El Greco, for he was an ardent student of the Italian masters, and like the Dutch he knew much about the texture of skin, hair, and cloth. See, for example, his *Portrait of a Young Man,* probably a courtier. He was famous for his perfect likenesses of his models, and

we cannot doubt that this is the picture of a bright, alert young man. We can also see one very interesting thing about Velásquez—he used what is called a "limited palette." By this we mean he did not use all the colors he could have put on his "palette," the board on which artists mix their paint. Velásquez liked tones of silvery gray, soft brown, and darker colors. This particularly suited the taste of the day, when men and women in Spain usually wore black, or other quiet and somber shades.

After the seventeenth century, the court of Spain declined in power and wealth, for less gold was coming from the New World. Spain had never developed any industries to compete with those of the other countries of Europe, and her soil was poor. It was a hundred years before the Spanish court had another really great painter, its last, and this was Francisco Goya (1746–1828), who worked at the end of the eighteenth and the beginning of the nineteenth century, and who was as strange in his way as El Greco had been in his. Goya did many portraits of the members of the Spanish court, which are not unusual except in that they are true to the point of unkindness, for they do not flatter their subjects. A caricature is a mocking portrait that exaggerates the features of a face; Goya's portraits are almost caricatures of the members of a court now famous for its cruelty. But he was not unkind in his portrait of Victor Guye, the nephew of a distinguished general whom Goya also painted. Here we have merely an innocent child with big dark eyes, a bit overdressed in the uniform of a page at court.

Goya, like Rembrandt, was noted for his etchings. In these we see strange scenes from Goya's tortured imagination, beasts and monsters meant to represent some moral good or evil. Such a picture is his engraving of a bullfight. He wants to show us the full cruelty of the bloody spectacle, as the grinning torero is about to plunge his sword into the back of one suffering bull, while another is being taunted by the picador. We cannot make out their faces, but we can feel the unkindness of the crowd, and although the picture is not in color,

The Divided Bull Ring, by Goya (1746–1828)

we can sense that the arena is drenched in blood.

Goya, in both his portraits and his etchings, seems to be criticizing a wicked world, and this may be because of the feeling of the times, for, although there was no revolution in Spain, the age in which he worked was an age of revolution throughout Europe, as we shall see in the next chapter.

Victor Guye, by Goya (1746–1828)

XVI

Art in France

During the early seventeenth century there were two important painters in France, and both went to Rome to study, for the French court was not yet important enough to attract artists. These men were Nicolas Poussin (1594–1665) and Claude Lorrain (1600–1682). Both were landscape painters, and landscape painting was very important at the time, if you remember the works of the Dutch masters we have seen. But Poussin and Lorrain were very different from Ruisdael, for while the Dutch artists painted landscapes as they really were, these two painted imaginary landscapes of great beauty. They were not meant to be paintings of the countryside of the day. Poussin and Lorrain were great admirers of Classical antiquity, which is why they preferred Rome to their native France, and so they put into their landscapes bits of architecture and figures to make them appear to represent Greek or Roman "pastoral" scenes, by which we mean scenes from the quiet lives of shepherds in the country. No view was ever so beautiful as that of Lorrain's *The Herdsman*. Behind the loll-

ing shepherd we see a countryside bathed in the golden light of a setting sun, the foreground clear and the background disappearing into a warm haze.

France, like Spain, had a strong central monarchy, and in 1643 there came to the throne a king of great importance. He was Louis XIV, and under him France rose to be the most important country in Europe and the French court became the most brilliant in the world. Louis and his successors, Louis XV and Louis XVI, who lived during the eighteenth century, were great patrons of the arts. They built many large and luxurious palaces, the equal of which were never seen before or since. Louis XIV's palace of Versailles is the largest in history. It is small wonder that Louis called himself the *Roi Soleil*, which means "Sun King," and we can get some idea of what he looked like from the bronze portrait bust of him by Giovanni Bernini (1598–1680), a great Italian sculptor and architect of the time. Notice how the hair and drapery swirl around Louis's haughty face. Bernini was a sculptor of the Baroque style we have already

The Herdsman, by Claude Lorrain (1600–1682)

Louis XIV, by Bernini (1598–1680)

seen in the paintings of Tintoretto and Rubens.

Many painters and sculptors were kept busy covering the walls of the palaces and beautiful "châteaux," or castles, of Louis's noblemen with paintings, and ornamenting their miles and miles of formal gardens with graceful statuary. The sculptors' favorite subjects were usually figures and scenes from Greek and Roman life and mythology, such as Clodion's statue of a vestal, a Roman priestess.

But painters often depicted the carefree life of the courtiers—beautiful maidens and handsome youths of the court amusing themselves at picnics, or watching theatrical performances, or playing at being shepherds and shepherdesses. At times they even used portraits of the king and members of the court as figures in their decorative designs. These paintings have often been criticized as being more "pretty" than "beautiful," and this may be because the French artists preferred delicate, soft lines, and "pretty" colors such as pale pink and blue, to the strong and majestic sweeps of reds, blues, and purples of the painters of the Italian Renaissance. This style is often called "Rococo."

The greatest of all these courtly painters was Antoine Watteau (1684–1721). Among his favorite subjects were the performances of the *com-*

media dell'arte, the traveling companies of Italian actors who put on little plays for the court, always using the same characters, such as Harlequin, a young trickster, and Columbine, a fair maiden. His *Italian Comedians* is a delicate Rococo painting of such a performance, full of soft lines and colors and graceful gestures.

The finest painter in the next generation was Francois Boucher (1703–1770), who was particularly well known for his portraits of ladies of the court. What a delightful decoration his painting of *Madame Bergeret* is. She seems to exist in a world of perfume, roses, and rustling silk. But perhaps the painter who most perfectly portrayed the leisurely and elegant dream-life of the courtiers was Jean Honoré Fragonard (1732–1806). He was particularly famous for his landscapes of soaring trees, bright blue skies, and puffy white clouds. The graceful figures in his painting *The Swing* are forever at play in an imaginary park. Such was

A Vestal, by Clodion (1738–1814)

Italian Comedians, by Watteau (1684–1721)

The Swing, by Fragonard (1732–1806)

Madame Bergeret, by Boucher (1703–1770)

Soap Bubbles, by Chardin (1699–1779)

the life of the French court in the eighteenth century, but it was not to go on forever.

There lived during this century, however, one painter who, like the Dutch masters, loved the simple home life of the people, and that was Jean Siméon Chardin (1699–1779). He particularly liked scenes of children at home—playing, eating their meals, or saying their prayers. His *Soap Bubbles* is such a picture. It is simply a painting of a boy sitting at a window blowing bubbles. His little brother is peeking over the edge of the sill to see how he is doing. Like those of the Dutch, Chardin's colors are darker and more somber, and his lines more simple, than those of the other French painters of his age.

Among the many sculptors that worked for the French court and nobility of the Louis', one was very great indeed: Jean Antoine Houdon (1741–1828). He is particularly famous for his portrait busts, which show not only the physical appearance but the character of the model. There was no artist at court who was as fine a portraitist with a brush as Houdon was in marble. His bust of Voltaire is particularly interesting, for Voltaire was the most famous wit and political thinker of the age, and Houdon has brought his genius to life in marble. It was Voltaire who foresaw the end of the *ancien régime,* the old way of life and government of the Louis', and the new liberty of the future, and who said, "I disapprove of what you say, but I will defend to the death your right to say it."

So it was at the court of the Louis', but its play could not go on forever. Suddenly, at the end of the eighteenth century, as Voltaire had foreseen, the dark cloud of revolution spread over France. The nobility seldom thought of sharing their wealth with the rest of the population, and the peasantry became violently jealous of the magnificence of the court. The middle class, which with the coming of modern industry was only now beginning to develop, was likewise displeased with the rules and regulations imposed by the court. In 1789 the storm broke. The people arose to the cry of revolution already successful in America, and marched on the palace of Versailles. They dug the very cobblestones up from the courtyard and

National Gallery of Art, Washington, D.C., Widener Collection

Voltaire, by Houdon (1741–1828)

smashed the windows. The King, Louis XVI, and his wife, Marie Antoinette, were hauled off to Paris and beheaded, along with a great number of the nobility. Then new groups came to power, and many leaders of the revolution themselves were led to the guillotine. France fell into complete confusion, and was not reorganized until there arose a young military officer from Corsica, Napoleon Bonaparte. Napoleon claimed to be establishing a republic such as that which existed in the Rome of the Senate, although in fact he was founding an empire like that of the Rome of Augustus, with himself as Emperor.

The French Revolution was not only a political revolution, but brought with it a revolution in art. Many of the beautiful palaces and châteaux of the *ancien régime* were destroyed, and the leisurely life of the aristocracy, which had inspired their painted and sculptural decorations, was gone forever. Nevertheless there were as many great artists in France after the Revolution as there had been before, and if their work was different, it was because they were working in a new age.

As we have seen, the followers of the Revolution and of Napoleon believed they were re-creating the rule of the people which had existed in ancient Rome, and so they tried, in their painting, sculpture, and architecture, to imitate what they felt to be "Roman." At this time buildings were erected with colonnades in imitation of the Roman Forum, and furniture was constructed according to Roman design, and decorated with figures such as the eagle, the symbol of the Roman Legions. Ladies gave up the great billowing skirts and tiny waists of the *ancien régime,* and wore something like the drapery of Roman women, while men's dress became much simpler. Nothing was to look as it had before. After Napoleon actually came to power this style was called "Empire," and the most famous painter of the Empire style was Jacques Louis David (1748–1825). David was the chief portraitist of the Revolution and later became court painter to Napoleon, often using the Emperor as his model. Apart from portraits, his favorite subjects were scenes from Classical mythology and the history of Greece and Rome. He painted with clean lines and soft colors, mostly blues and grays, so that his figures looked like Roman statuary.

David's portrait of Napoleon in his study is particularly interesting. Napoleon is painted in the uniform of the Imperial Guard, wearing the epaulets of a general, and the insignia of the Legion of Honor. But look closely at the objects in his study. The clock reads almost 4:15, but it is not late afternoon, for the room is dark, and the candle on the desk is burning low—it is 4:15 in the morning! The desk is covered with papers—the Emperor has been hard at work until the early hours. It is told that when he saw this picture Napoleon said to the painter, "You have understood me, David. By night I work for the welfare of my subjects, and by day for their glory."

But the Empire, too, came to an end. Napoleon tried to quiet the confused state of affairs at home by leading the armies of France to the conquest of all Europe, and he almost succeeded. But he became too ambitious. He marched into Russia and got as far as Moscow. Then the Russian winter came, and with it cold and disease that destroyed his army. Despite this, he drew together a new force. When he was finally defeated at Waterloo in 1815 by an alliance of his enemies abroad, his enemies at home came to power, and his rule was ended.

After Napoleon, a more truly democratic government was established in France, and there was still another revolution in art. There were fewer palaces and great public buildings to decorate, and therefore less demand for statuary. As had happened in Holland centuries earlier, the new patrons of art were businessmen and members of the middle class, who wanted paintings for their simple but tasteful homes. And so, during the nineteenth century in France, we often find paintings of quiet country scenes and of the life of the peasants. This is particularly true of the works of the painters of the "Barbizon school," such as Camille Corot (1796-1875).

Their work is said to be of the "Barbizon school" because they formed a colony of artists, a group of painters working together, in the quiet country village of Barbizon, only a few miles from Paris. Barbizon has been preserved to this day much as it was in the nineteenth century, and if you are interested, you can take a bus from Paris, through fields that might still serve as a background for the paintings of the school, to the very village itself, where you may still find the restful calm of such works as Corot's peaceful country view, *Ville d'Avray,* a picture of his father's home outside Paris.

This taste for scenes of peasant life was part of a desire felt by many in the nineteenth century to "escape" their humdrum city lives, and this movement was called "Romanticism." There arose in literature and painting another kind of "escape" as well: an interest in strange and faraway places, and in little-known corners of history. People were fascinated by North Africa and the East, which were now, for the first time, open to the visits of

Napoleon in His Study, by David (1748–1825)

Ville d'Avray, by Corot (1796–1875)

adventurous travelers, as well as to ambitious colonists. What tales were flooding Europe! The French armies had gone with Napoleon to Egypt, and the English had conquered India. Adventurers like Richard Burton were making the pilgrimage to Mecca, forbidden to all but Moslems; and Stanley was searching the African jungle for that elderly gentleman, Dr. Livingstone, who spent many years discovering the strange habits of the unknown tribesmen and mapping territory never before seen by a European. The "Romantics" liked exciting scenes from the lives of the Arabs and the Turks, stories from history and the Bible, and the adventures of the Crusades and the early explorers. The greatest of the French Romantic painters was Eugène Delacroix (1799–1863). His pictures, such as *The Magyar Horseman,* are usually full of gusto, color, and motion, with quick brush strokes very different from the cold, hard lines of David. His painting of *Columbus and His Son at La Rabida* is quieter than most of his works, but it shows Delacroix's interest in re-creating a scene that occurred four hundred years before his day as much

as it might actually have looked as possible. Delacroix has painted the arrival of Columbus with his son at the monastery of La Rabida in Spain, where he stopped and was aided in his search for a patron to finance his voyage to the New World. The scene is a quiet and somber one, in the mood of Columbus' discouragement, and Delacroix chose a room in a well-known Spanish monastery of Columbus' own day to use a model for his background. The costumes of the figures are also those of the year 1492. This is because the viewers of Delacroix's painting wanted to be transported into the past when they looked at his picture. How unlike the men of the Renaissance, such as Tintoretto, who painted all scenes from history, mythology, and the Bible as if they were taking place in the Italy of their own day.

In art, France was the most important country in the world in the nineteenth century, as it had been in the eighteenth, and it was here, as we shall see, that the last and most important revolution in the history of art took place.

The Magyar Horseman, by Delacroix (1798–1863)

XVII

Art in England

So great was the art of Italy and France that the English felt for a long time that all good painting and sculpture must come from one of these lands, and that nothing done in their country could compare with it. And so it was not until the eighteenth century that there were any great painters in England.

What was England like in the eighteenth century? There was no gay court life to be painted. The king of England was not as important in his own country as were the kings of France and Spain, for many of his powers had been taken from him in the revolution of the Puritans under Cromwell a century before. The nobles lived not at court around the king but in their own beautiful manor houses on their country estates, where they spent their lives pleasantly, hunting and fishing. Meanwhile the cities were crowded and bustling, for the English were beginning to conquer distant peoples and establish colonies, and the port of London was crowded with ships laden with goods from India and China in the east and the Americas in the west.

William Hogarth (1697–1764), the son of a poor London schoolmaster, was the first artist to try to prove that an Englishman could paint as well as a foreigner. As a boy, he wandered through the streets of London, and all his life he loved to paint the simple people and busy life he saw there. So it was that his subjects were always English, even though he studied the Italian masters with great care and used their style. As a child, he may have saved up his pennies to buy shrimps from girls like the one he painted years later, a typical London street vendor.

What the English wanted most of all were portraits of themselves and their children to hang in their gracious country homes. Even the wealthiest and most noble thought of themselves as plain country people, and they liked to be shown in dress much simpler than the silks and bows of the French courtiers, and posed before a lovely English landscape.

Look at *Master John Heathcote*. Perhaps he has just been for a walk in the damp autumn countryside we see behind him. In any case, there he

119

Columbus and His Son at La Rabida, by Delacroix (1799–1863)

Miss Willoughby, by Romney (1734–1802)

Master John Heathcote, by Gainsborough (1727–1788)

stands, simply, holding some posies he has just picked. The story is told that Master Heathcote's parents had lost all their other children, and for this reason were most anxious to have a fine portrait of the one who remained to them. At first

The Shrimp Girl, by Hogarth (1697–1764)

Thomas Gainsborough (1727–1788), who painted this picture, felt he was too busy to do a portrait of Master Heathcote, but upon hearing this sad story he agreed to it. When the parents brought their child, the artist was delighted with the simple white dress and blue sash he was wearing (small boys were dressed in this way at that time), and said, "You have brought him simply dressed. Had you paraded him in fancy costume, I would not have painted him." Gainsborough was typical of the first great English portrait painters to be accepted and admired throughout the world, and the most important people in England flocked to his studio. They came to Sir Joshua Reynolds (1723–1792) as well. He was the son of a Devon-

shire schoolteacher who thought him lazy and worthless. When he was twenty-three he went to study painting under a master, and then to Italy to see the great works of the Renaissance; and when he returned, he became one of the most successful portrait artists of his day.

There were other fine portrait painters in England in the eighteenth century as well, such as Sir Henry Raeburn (1756–1823), the famous Scottish artist, and George Romney (1734–1802), who painted the charming Miss Willoughby. A carpenter's son, Romney went off to Italy and came back, like Reynolds, to be a great success in London. In the next century, their tradition was continued by Sir Thomas Lawrence (1769–1830). He was the son of an innkeeper, and so clever was he at drawing that he was already selling pictures when he was ten years old.

All of these painters loved to portray the blue, wind-blown sky of their native land, and the fresh cheeks of women and children. And what experts they were! You can almost feel the taffeta of Master Heathcote's sash.

Because the English loved the country, they loved landscape painting, and the two greatest landscape painters of the nineteenth century were both English. Like Corot and the Barbizon painters, they are artists of the Romantic movement. John Constable (1776–1837) painted the twisted trees and sunny meadows of a perfect England. In fact, so true are his works to the English countryside as it still is, that his *View of Salisbury Cathedral* might have been painted yesterday.

The works of William Turner (1775–1851) were quite different. Like Lorrain and Poussin, he painted dream landscapes of ideal beauty, and he loved to fill them with a misty golden haze. Such a picture is his *Keelmen Heaving In Coals by Moonlight*. The ships are suggested with a few lines, hidden in the dark smudges of smoke that rise from the coal fires, and the whole scene is bathed in the soft light of the moon. Turner had a great influence on later painters, as we shall see.

A View of Salisbury Cathedral, by Constable (1776–1837)

XVIII

Art in America

Do not think that while so much was going on in Europe there was no art in America. No matter where men are, they always want to paint and sculpt the life they see around them and feel within.

The very earliest settlers in America, though, had very little time to think of art. Making a livelihood in the wild new country was struggle enough. There were no schools of art, and Europe was very far away indeed—weeks and months of storm-tossed seas lay between America and the ports of the Old World. All the colonists had to remind them of the art they had left behind were a few paintings, mostly family portraits, that some of the wealthier settlers had brought with them. And yet, among the early comers to the eastern colonies and the pioneers who pushed further west, there were men who wanted to paint the new and exciting world around them, things never before seen by white men—the strange dress and customs of the American Indians, the stampeding buffalo of the plains. Then too, families in America, as in

Europe, wanted portraits by which they might remember their loved ones. These early painters in America were largely self-taught men. They had few models from Europe, as we have seen, and they had to struggle with many of the problems that the painters of Europe had solved centuries before. So it is that their paintings, like that of *Mrs. Freake and Baby Mary,* a typical colonial woman and her child, may seem flat and stiff, their proportions and perspective incorrect. For this reason they are called "American Primitives." Their work often looks like that of a primitive people just learning to draw. Still, many of their pictures, such as that of Mrs. Freake, are full of charm and life.

By the end of colonial days America had come much closer to Europe. There was regular travel, and a young man who wanted to be a painter in America could study with some master, possibly from Europe, or travel abroad and study in a foreign capital. Until the Revolution the American colonies were under British rule in art as well as in politics. Young Americans went to study with

Keelmen Heaving In Coals by Moonlight, by Turner (1775–1851)

National Gallery of Art, Washington, D.C., Widener Collection

Mrs. Freake and Baby Mary, American Primitive

the great English portraitists and copied their style. In fact, John Singleton Copley (1738–1815), one of the finest painters in the colonies, was a loyalist, and fled to England at the outbreak of the Revolution, while Benjamin West (1738–1820), another American, spent his whole career in London and was considered one of the finest painters in England. Here we see Copley's painting of his

126

The Copley Family, by Copley (1738–1815)

Breezing Up,
by Homer (1836–1910)

own family shortly after their arrival in England. The young man at the back of the picture is the painter himself, seen with his wife, his four children, and his father-in-law. If this elderly gentleman seems like a stern and troubled man, he has good reason to be, for he is the very man whose consignment of tea was thrown into Boston Harbor by the Revolutionaries in the famous "Boston Tea Party."

The best-known of the American painters of the day, and one of the finest portraitists of his time, Gilbert Stuart (1755–1828), remained in the United States after the Revolution and painted many portraits of George Washington. In fact, you will be surprised to learn that several of these are in the great collections of England! Of course, he too had been brought up in the English colonies and painted in the style of Gainsborough and Reynolds, and he made frequent visits to England. During one such trip he agreed to paint the portrait of an English gentleman, but the day of the sitting was so cold that when his subject arrived he remarked that it was a better day for skating than for painting, and so painter and model set off for a pond in the park. The result was Stuart's picture *The Skater,* perhaps the only portrait ever done of a man on ice skates!

After the Revolution, the artists of America turned away from England and towards France. Among the American painters most influenced by the French was Samuel F. B. Morse (1791–1872). Is that name familiar to you? It might well be—Morse is the very man who invented the telegraph!

I have already told you about the Romantic painters of nineteenth-century France and England, and how they loved to paint the simple life of the peasant, or strange scenes from the past or faraway places. There were Romantics in America too—especially in America, for nature was closer to American painters of a hundred years ago than it was to the artists of Europe, and they loved to paint the typical scenes of their wild new country as they saw them. Winslow Homer (1836–1910) was a great artist of the wilderness and the people who inhabited it—hunters, trappers, and traders. He was brought up on the coast of New England, and he painted again and again the angry sea and the struggles of the Atlantic fisherman. No one in the nineteenth century could paint a thick green forest or a foamy sea as well as he, and *Breezing Up* is a good example of his work—four boys in an open boat under a brisk wind, in the dim sunlight of a New England afternoon.

But the greatest American Romantic was Albert Pinkham Ryder (1847–1917). Born the son of fisherfolk in New Bedford, Massachusetts, Ryder decided to become a painter when just a boy, and his family allowed him to study, first in New Bedford and then in New York. In fact, he spent almost his entire life in a tiny apartment in Man-

129

The Skater, by Gilbert Stuart (1755–1828)

Detail of Siegfried and the Rhine Maidens, by Ryder (1847–1917)

The White Girl, by Whistler (1834–1903)

hattan. Ryder painted landscapes and seascapes, and scenes taken from ancient myths and legends and the plays of Shakespeare. But how strange these pictures are! Even the subjects that might seem familiar, such as an orchard or a cow in a pasture, seem to be seen in a hazy dream. Ryder especially loved to paint mysterious, shadowy figures seen by moonlight, and no painter ever captured the magic of moonlight so well. Look at Siegfried, the hero of German mythology, riding along the banks of the Rhine on a windy and moonlit night. Ryder saw this scene in his imagination, and when we look at it, we feel as if we see it in our own.

Towards the end of the nineteenth century, a great change happened in European art, and we shall learn about it in the next chapter. This was "Impressionism," and it had some influence on James McNeill Whistler (1834–1903), an American painter who, unlike Homer and Ryder, was a great portraitist and famous throughout Europe.

Whistler painted graceful pictures in soft tones, and he was particularly interested in carefully arranged compositions. In fact, the title he gave his famous portrait of his mother was simply *Arrangement in Grey and Black,* and his *White Girl,* a portrait of a famous beauty who also posed for Courbet, might just as well be called *Arrangement in White.* He wanted it to be known that it was the composition of his painting, and not its subject, that was important. In what way Whistler was like the Impressionists you will best be able to tell when you have read about them.

Nor must we think that America was without her sculptors. Augustus Saint-Gaudens (1848–1907), the son of an immigrant family, half Irish and half French, was one of the great sculptors of the century. After he had studied at the finest schools of art in the United States, he went to France and then Italy. But he remained always truly American, as we can tell from the subject of the first work he chose to exhibit in Paris—a statue of Hiawatha. He returned to America after a few years of study abroad, and was much appreciated for the strength and dignity of his sculpture. In fact, there are handsome monuments by Saint-Gaudens from one end of the country to the other. His portrait of Admiral David Farragut is a good example of his work. It brings to life all the fire and strength of that salty hero of the Civil War.

Admiral David Farragut, by Saint-Gaudens (1848–1907)

XIX
New Ideas

You might go to a museum today and see a picture that consists entirely of splashes and lines of color, like the work of the modern painter Vassily Kandinsky (1866–1944). You will probably wonder how, in so short a time, styles of painting could have changed so very much, for Delacroix died less than three years before Kandinsky was born. Art seems to have changed more in the past century than it had from the time of the tombs of the Pharaohs, five thousand years ago, or even from the age of the cave painters, sixty thousand years ago! Suddenly, the subject of a painting is no longer important. There doesn't need to be any subject at all! How did this happen? You will be amazed to learn that this change actually started with a group of painters who wanted to show more truly what they saw with their eyes. This last and greatest revolution in the history of art happened, as I have told you, in France.

The first painter to break away was Gustave Courbet (1819–1877). Courbet felt that the only true subject for the painter is everyday life as it is actually seen. He hated alike the posed, cold figures of the Empire school and Delacroix's strange and wild scenes of faraway times and places. Once, when asked to paint a religious subject, he laughed and said, "Show me an angel, and I will paint one." He felt that a portrait of himself taking an afternoon walk in the country would be far more real to the viewer. Or he would paint a group of stonecutters in a quarry as we see here, not gracefully posed, like Millet's peasants, but in any awkward gesture in which we might catch them off guard, at a glance. Notice how the picture seems to have been painted in broad daylight, and how everything the workmen are wearing is painted just as it might be seen—their rumpled white shirts and ill-fitting clogs.

Courbet was followed by a younger man, Edouard Manet (1832–1883), who also believed that the real world as one would catch it at a glance is the only subject for painting. But Manet was particularly interested in capturing the bright sunlight that we see out of doors. You have surely

The Stonecutters, by Courbet (1819–1877)

noticed that when you look into the sunlit air, everything is so brilliant that it almost hurts your eyes, and you cannot look for long. Manet wanted to bring this light onto his canvas, and no painter had ever done this before. Now, have you ever looked at a tree in the sun? Do you see every separate leaf? No, you do not; you see many tiny blotches of color that blend into each other, and the total effect is green. This is particularly true of everything we see in a bright light. What is more, the blotches of color are not, necessarily, what we expect. Shadows are not merely darker shades of the same color, but different colors, and often filled with colors reflected from other objects. Of course, painters before Manet had experimented with light on objects, and had noticed these things. This was especially true of the Venetian Titian, as we have seen, and of Turner, whose painted landscapes are full of warm light. You

must know the rhyme about the purple cow. Well, Turner once said, when he saw a black cow standing before a brilliant setting sun, "She is not black—she is purple!" We often do not realize these tricks that light plays on us, and we think we see what we expect to see, but Manet felt that he should try to put light on his canvases exactly as the eye saw it. If we look at his paintings from close at hand, we just see flat spots and splashes of bright color; but if we step back, what a sight meets our eyes! Brilliant light fills the scene as it had never before in painting.

Manet's *Gare Saint-Lazare* is not a picture of Saint-Lazare railroad station in Paris at all; it is the picture of a mother and child at an iron fence in front of the tracks. We see no steam engine, but one is suggested by the great, bright cloud of steam behind the fence. Look closely at the picture. The girl's bow, her hair, the steam, trees,

*Gare Saint-Lazare,
by Manet (1832–1883)*

house behind the fence—all are made up of splashes of paint, but if we look quickly at the picture we have no doubt of what is there; it is all very real. Look at the sleeping puppy in the mother's lap—only a few strokes of brown and white paint, but we know that he is a warm, sleepy puppy; and there can be no question that the houses behind the track are at some distance from the bars of the fence. Manet was very successful at the effect of depth in his new style of painting.

Manet and his friends and followers who experimented with the painting of light in this way were called "Impressionists" because they tried to paint a moment's "impression" of light and color on the eye. Among the greatest of the Impressionists was Claude Monet (1840–1926). Monet was a poor young man with the strong belief that a painter must work out of doors. Therefore he turned a tiny houseboat into a studio, and traveled along the River Seine in search of scenes to paint, such as *The Banks of the Seine at Vetheuil*. The mass of daisies and dandelions, the water beyond, and the trees on the opposite banks are only a riot of patches of color until we step back, and then the cheerful river scene floats mistily before our eyes.

Do not think, though, that the Impressionists were interested only in landscapes and the effect of light on the surfaces of things. Auguste Renoir (1841–1919) and Edgar Degas (1834–1917) used the techniques of the Impressionists to paint charming portraits and studies of people. Renoir

A Girl with a Watering Can, by Renoir (1841–1919)

loved to paint scenes of dancing and revelry, and beautiful women and children, fresh and healthy, with pink cheeks and large eyes, like his *Girl with a Watering Can*. Degas was particularly interested in capturing the effect of movement with one quick stroke of the brush. He liked to set up his easel in a ballet-school practice room, or at the races, as we see here. Degas has tried to do something not done by the Impressionists before except for Renoir. He tried not only to paint people and animals but to put them into motion, and he succeeded very well. His horses and jockeys may be only faint splotches of color on an overcast day, but they do appear to scamper around the field, and the picture is full of motion.

When the paintings of the Impressionists first appeared, the public was shocked. Galleries in which paintings could be seen by the public (and bought, too) were something new in the nineteenth century, but by the time of the Impressionists it was the common way, as it is today, for a painter's work to become known. When the official galleries refused to show their works, the Impressionists banded together to give themselves a showing in what they called "The Gallery of the Rejected." With what jeers they were greeted! Lunatics! Disasters! That is what the critics called the Impressionists and their paintings. And it is not surprising, considering how different they were from what the public was used to. None the less, they were gradually accepted, and followed by the finest painters of the next generation.

The greatest sculptor of the ninteenth century, Auguste Rodin (1840–1917), was also what might be called an Impressionist. He tried to capture the impression that an object gave at a certain moment. His knowledge of anatomy was as great as Michelangelo's, but, like the Impressionists, he experimented. How does a man actually look when walking? We know that when one foot is on the ground, the other is slightly raised, but do we see this with our eyes? Or is the motion too fast for our eyes to catch? How can the sculptor give the impression of a walking figure? See Rodin's *Saint John the Baptist Preaching*. Never has the simple motion of walking been so perfectly portrayed. But see—both feet are squarely on the ground! Notice too, that Rodin has not carefully modeled every hair on the head of his figure. He has somehow captured the impression of light and dark patches that hair makes on the eye. But didn't Praxiteles do this too? He did, as we have seen, for impressionism is not really new in art, although it had never been so carefully studied before.

But, you will say, the Impressionists are still painting and sculpturing men and women, country scenes, and such, just as before. What is more, they are trying to make them appear more real than ever. What has all this to do with pictures

The Banks of the Seine at Vetheuil, by Monet (1840–1926)

National Gallery of Art, Washington, D.C., Chester Dale Collection

that are only shapes and forms, that have no subject? Wait, and you shall see.

In 1839 there was born in the south of France a man named Paul Cézanne, the son of a wealthy banker. Young Cézanne was determined to be a great Impressionist painter, but he felt the Impressionists had made some mistakes. The outline, the shape of objects, was lost in their many brightly colored brush strokes. What is more, their pictures seemed to have no design, or what we have called "composition"—that is, the pleasing placement of shapes within the picture. Cézanne set about to bring these back into painting. He would paint a subject as simple as a bowl of fruit over and over again, using the tiny patches of color of the Impressionists, until the apples seemed very solid and firm, and their placement on the table made a perfect composition. In fact, Cézanne was so interested in the correct placement of objects in his pictures and the lovely patterns made by their outlines that he would sometimes distort their shape. He would paint a bowl that seemed not quite round, or a table that seemed to be tipped forward, as, for example, in the *Still Life* we see here. As we have seen, El Greco did this, but not as much as did Cézanne. In trying to show the Impressionist painters how they could give their pictures composition, he had made design more important than it had ever been considered before.

While Cézanne was painting at his home in Aix-en-Provence, there was still another great painter working in the south of France; his name was Vincent van Gogh (1853–1890). Van Gogh was the poor son of a Dutch vicar, and he had himself worked as a preacher among the impoverished Belgian miners. He was a very religious man, and a very unhappy one. Van Gogh painted the countryside and the simple lives and homes of the peasants in the most brilliant colors ever used by any painter. Like Cézanne, and the Impressionists, he painted with splashes of color, but his brush strokes seem twisted and tortured. When we look at his picture *The Olive Orchard,* we can almost feel the excitement the painter must have felt when he saw the whirling, brilliant sunlight on

Collection, The Museum of Modern Art, New York, Mrs. Simon Guggenheim Fund

Saint John the Baptist Preaching, by Rodin (1840–1917)

the gnarled trees. Van Gogh, too, distorted his figures and objects to make a perfect composition, and, as did El Greco, to make us feel a certain way.

And there was still another painter to whom design, patterns of color, were even more important than to Cézanne and Van Gogh. This was Paul Gauguin (1848–1903), a close friend of Van Gogh. Gauguin was just a French businessman, leading a very ordinary life, but he became interested in painting, so interested that he felt he must give up

The Races, by Degas (1834–1917)

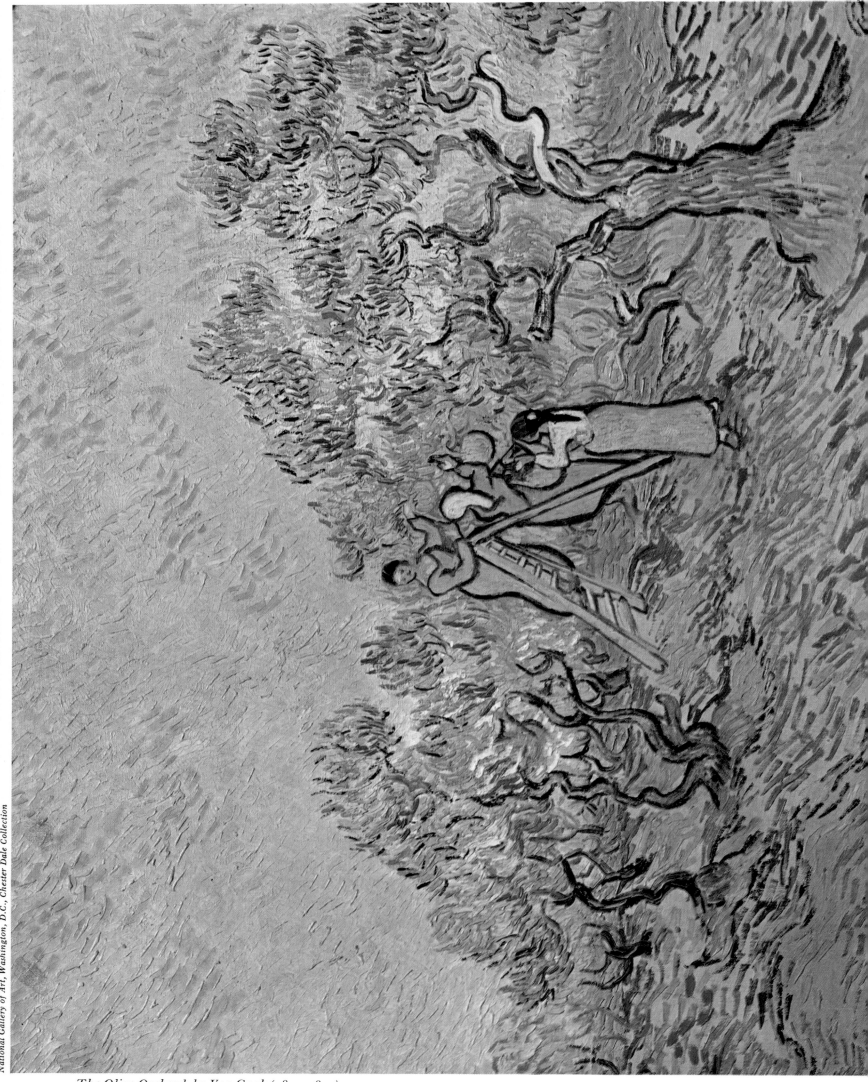

The Olive Orchard, by Van Gogh (1853–1890)

Still Life, by Cézanne (1839–1906)

his occupation, and then life in civilized Europe altogether. He thought that if he could flee to the primitive world, he could paint life more simply, as he felt it to be hidden beneath the cover of learning and the rules of behavior in the Western world. And so Gauguin went to Tahiti, where he lived with the natives as one of them, and painted their way of life. His pictures are swirling patterns of flat color like *Fatata Te Miti,* which is Tahitian for "By the Sea." The figures of the bathers may seem drawn in a childish way, but this is not important, for they are part of a pattern, and no more important than any other part, just as men in the jungle are part of nature.

The young painters who studied and admired the work of Cézanne and Van Gogh felt that the shape of things and the design they formed, or the feeling or emotion that they gave those who looked at them, were most important in any picture. This meant that objects sometimes had to be distorted until they could hardly be recognized and merely suggested what they were meant to represent.

In *The Cry,* by Edward Munch (1863-1944), the strong emotion that we feel is the terror of a scream. Munch was one of the first of a group of painters called "Expressionists" who wanted to "express" overpowering emotions in their works. *The Cry* is a mysterious painting, and we cannot guess the reasons for the fear. Yet the whirling lines of the sky, the gesture of the figure, and the terrible circle of its lips tell us there is reason to fear, and we can almost hear the scream itself.

Fatata Te Miti,
by Gauguin (1848–1903)

The Lovers is a work by Pablo Picasso (1881-1973), the Spaniard who was perhaps the greatest artist of our century. The figures have been drawn in simple outline, with very little attention to anatomy, and then filled in with flat color, almost without shading. Still, there are other things to notice: the beauty of Picasso's rippling line, and the lovely combination of surfaces of color—red, yellow, green, blue, and purple. But above all, there is the feeling of affection between the two people—the concerned look of the young man, the shy gaze of the girl. We can feel it much more strongly than many emotions we have seen in paintings that were much closer to the reality of a photograph.

Picasso painted and sculpted in many styles. He and his friend, Georges Braque (1892-1967), experimented together, breaking down the objects which they painted into angular planes. Placed one on top of the other, these planes, which are sometimes transparent, seem to create patterns that move in space. Braque's painting entitled *Still Life: Le Jour* portrays a table with a copy of the newspaper *Le Jour,* some apples, a knife, a pipe, a mandolin, and a jug. But we scarcely notice any of these things. What we see is the powerful composition itself, made up of planes that look like many blocks or cubes. This manner of painting became known, therefore, as "Cubism."

A group of young painters soon felt strongly that it was not necessary to paint any subject at all. If we look at a gray sky, with a huge thundercloud in it, we feel sad, or perhaps frightened, as we do when we look at the sky in *The Cry*. But what makes us feel this way? Surely it is nothing more than the shapes and colors we see in the sky. And so shapes and colors alone can give us feelings, even if they represent nothing that we can name. One of the first artists to think this way was Wassily Kandinsky (1866-1944). In his *Composition Number 3* we may see exciting and interesting shapes that make us feel a certain way, perhaps gay and happy, although we cannot actually say why. Such art is called "abstract" because the artist has "abstracted" the lines and shapes he has seen in nature to create a pure pattern of color.

If we compare *Broadway Boogie Woogie*, by the Dutch artist Piet Mondrian (1872-1944), with Kandinsky's painting, we notice how different abstract painters see the world in very different ways. Mondrian's painting is all squares, right angles, and clear, flat surfaces. And yet it does suggest to us the blinking lights, busy crisscrossing streets, and geometric shapes of a big city.

Sculptors, too, work solid materials into forms that might or might not suggest some figure or object. *Bird in Space,* by Constantin Brancusi (1876-1957), could hardly be called a statue of a bird, but its soaring grace gives us the sensation of flight much more strikingly than would an actual figure of a bird, with every feather carefully modeled.

As we can see, artists have had great freedom in the twentieth century to paint and sculpt in new and different ways. The "Surrealists," for example, painted objects with the absolute realism we have seen in the art of earlier centuries. And yet paintings like *Time Transfixed* by René Magritte (1898-1967) look very strange to us. This is not because of the way the Surrealists chose to paint, but because of what they painted. The Surrealists wanted to re-create the strange world of our dreams. We all

The Cry, by Munch (1863–1944)

*The Lovers,
by Picasso (1881–1973)*

know that when we dream, we see objects that are familiar to us in everyday life. What is unfamiliar is the setting in which we find them, or the role they play in our dreams. So, in *Time Transfixed,* a steam engine, to our amazement, comes chugging and smoking out of a fireplace. As in a dream, everything is out of scale. Either the fireplace is too large, or the train too small. The room itself appears at first very ordinary, but it seems strange, too. With its uncovered floorboards, its empty candlesticks, its blank mirror, its blocked fireplace, and its motionless clock, it is very bare, and this bareness haunts us. Only the train bursts through with life, and time does seem stopped or "transfixed." Such visions speak to us from our own dreams.

They are the key to our deepest thoughts and imaginings. They are more than merely realistic, they are "Surrealistic," a word which means "superrealistic."

During the nineteenth century and the early twentieth century, France led the world in art. Paris remained the center of ideas, a home where artists congregated, even though France was shaken by World War I. But at the time of World War II, many artists fled Europe and came to America. Working in the United States, they were a great inspiration to young American painters. During the 1940s and 1950s these artists developed a new movement of their own, and America became a leader in world art.

141

Composition Number 3, by Kandinsky (1866–1944)

143

Still Life: Le Jour, by Braque (1892–1967)

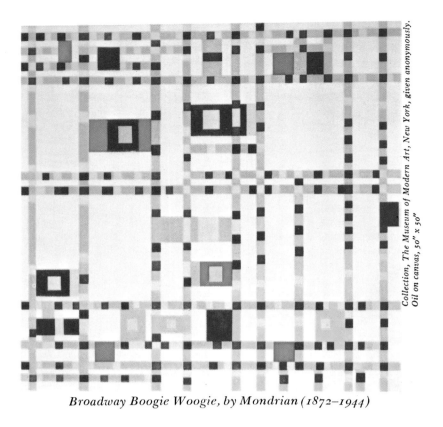

Collection, The Museum of Modern Art, New York, given anonymously.
Oil on canvas, 50" x 50"

Broadway Boogie Woogie, by Mondrian (1872–1944)

These young Americans were sometimes called "the New York School" because many of them lived and worked in New York. They were also called "Abstract Expressionists" because their paintings were "abstract," and also "expressed" intense feelings. In a way, Kandinsky was just such a painter. The works of the artists of the New York School do not resemble one another. Each artist had his own style, but all had one thing in common: the way that they painted. They did not plan their works. Jackson Pollock (1912-1956) felt that each painting had a life of its own. "I try to let it come through," he wrote. Pollock would place his canvas on the floor and paint with his whole body, dribbling and throwing layer upon layer of paint on the canvas, letting each pattern that was formed suggest the next, each one a gesture of emotion from his hand. The painting called *One (Number 31, 1950)* suggests one united whole. It is a pattern of light and shadow that seems very deep, so that we feel if we plunged into it we could not find the end.

The American, Alexander Calder (born in 1898), brought something new to abstract sculpture—

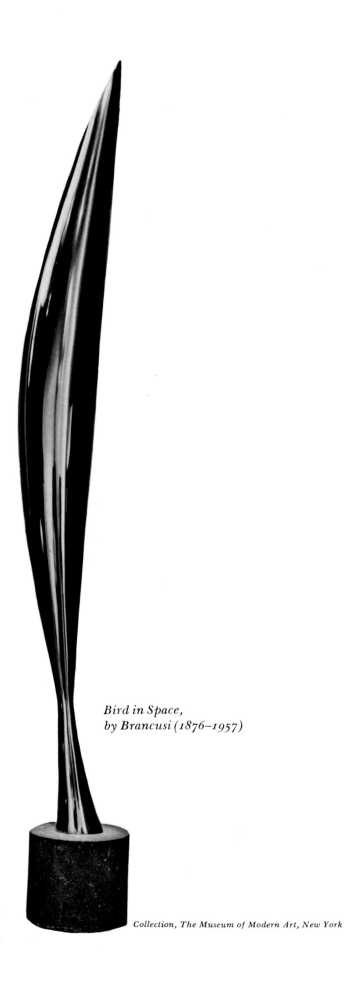

Bird in Space,
by Brancusi (1876–1957)

Collection, The Museum of Modern Art, New York

144

One (Number 31, 1950),
by Pollock (1912–1956)

Collection, The Museum of Modern Art, New York, gift of Sidney Janis. Oil and enamel 8' 10" x 17' 5⅝"

Time Transfixed, by Magritte (1898–1967)

145

Crag with Yellow Boomerang and Red Eggplant, by Calder (born in 1898)

movement. He was the son and grandson of sculptors, and had worked as a logger and engineer when he began to create sculptures in wire, made up of many independent parts. He discovered that by suspending his abstract shapes on wire from the ceiling or from a support, he could fashion "mobiles," as they came to be called, sculptures that could be made to move by the force of gravity and the motion of air alone. Just as there is an element of chance in the compositions of the Abstract Expressionist painters, so Calder's mobiles move to form new patterns by the chance of a sudden draft of air. Let us look at a sculpture called *Crag with Yellow Boomerang and Red Eggplant.* The "crag" is a "stabile," an unmoving form that sets squarely on the ground, and which looks like a craggy mountain. It supports a delightful, whimsical flurry of mobiles. If you look you will find the "yellow boomerang" and the "red eggplant" among them.

But not all recent American art is abstract art. You may walk into a museum and find yourself face to face with something you recognize very well, a large floppy hamburger. This is an example of what is called "Pop" Art. Like the Surrealists, the Pop Artists show us objects that are very real. But these are not visions that we might see in a dream. Instead, they are things we see every day of our lives, and so do not notice. They are taken from the "commercial" world of stores, food stands, movies, magazines, and shopping centers. The Pop Artist is telling us not to let our eyes pass over them, but to look at these objects very carefully. They are what our lives are made of. If we decide that they are ugly, then we have made for ourselves a very ugly world. Or perhaps we will feel that works of art such as *Soft Pay-Telephone* by Claes Oldenburg (born in 1929), a sculpture made of vinyl stuffed

with kapok, and then mounted on a painted wood panel, have a beauty all their own. Oldenburg wanted to create an art "as sweet and stupid as life itself." In any case the "Pop" Artist, who shows us what we see "popularly" around us, has made us look.

Abstract Expressionism and Pop Art are just a few of the many movements in the art of our day. The artists of the twentieth century, the followers of Cézanne, Van Gogh, and the Impressionists, experiment with many ways of showing us the world around us and the feelings within us, and of creating pictures and sculpture we enjoy looking at. These works may seem to you very different from the earlier art at which we have looked, but notice how very much the Byzantine Madonna differs from Raphael's beautiful painting of the same subject. And yet, both give us a feeling of solemnity and grandeur. If you think about this, it will help you understand how the art of our day approaches reality in its own way.

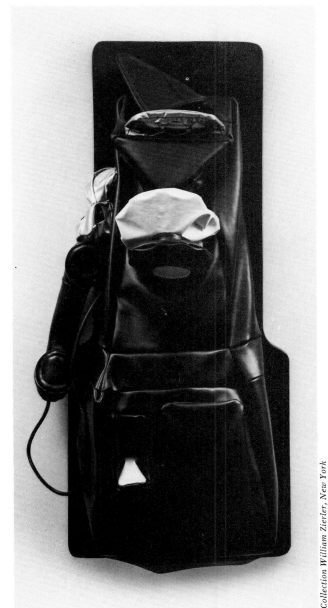

Soft Pay-Telephone,
by Oldenburg (born in 1929)

All Peoples Have Their Art

I have been telling you the history of the painting and sculpture of Europeans, and of Americans who are descended from Europeans, for this is the art that we most see around us. But all the peoples of the world have their art. Let us look, for example, at the work of the natives of Asia, Africa, and the South Seas.

The art of the countries that make up the Orient, or eastern part of the world, by which we mean the continent of Asia, reaches as far back into time as does the art of the West, which is what we have been studying in the pages of this book. The making of pictures and statues has been going on there for just as long, or nearly as long, and so you might think that there have been as many changes and developments in Oriental art as there have been in Western art. In fact, however, this is not at all the case. There are several important reasons for this.

First, we need to think of the differences between life in Asia and life in the West. Over the ages, the way of life in the countries of the East has changed very little. The peoples of Asia went

on being ruled by emperors, who had luxurious courts and who were often tyrants, long after the sort of life and work that we think of as slavery had begun to come to an end in the West. When things are this way, art is a luxury. It is made at the center of things, the court or city, to please a small number of people who have wealth and are educated to appreciate it.

Secondly, the East has always had its own religions, different from the Christianity that is the religion of the West. Even today, when the two parts of the world are much less cut off from one another than they once were, they are still far apart in their religious beliefs. Large parts of India, for example, have always held to the religion of Buddha, and therefore a great deal of the art of India over the ages has consisted of statues and paintings of the god Buddha and the decoration of temples meant for his worship. In China there is the religion of Confucius, a great teacher who is practically unknown in the West. In parts of India and Persia and in most of North Africa, the

Head of Buddha, Indian, 1st to 3rd Century A.D.

people are Mohammedans and follow the religious teachings of the prophet Mohammed. If you think of how much of the Western art that you have looked at in this book is built around persons and stories from the Bible and Christian religion, you will quickly see that Eastern art must be very different, not only in the subjects of its pictures and statues, but also in the way the people feel about works of art.

Lastly, the peoples of the East have always led a slower and quieter life than the peoples of the West. They have always had different and often much more strict rules of behavior, and where mechanical inventions or changes in dress or ideas about running a city are concerned, the clock of civilization has moved forward much more slowly than in Europe. Any visitor to the East today will

see people living as they have for hundreds of years, dressing the same way, eating the same foods, reading the same books, and believing the same things. And their art has changed little throughout their history. When a true Chinese craftsman makes a pot or a jar, he makes it as generations of his ancestors have done before him, and he makes it with a kind of religious devotion, letting all his thoughts and feelings become absorbed in the work, and trying to make them come out in the beauty of the finished object. This may be hard for us to imagine, but we must make the effort all the same.

In the Mohammedan, or Moslem, world, the religious laws have always forbidden the making of holy pictures and statues. Their God, they feel, is too holy to be shown before human eyes. As a result Moslem artists and craftsmen do not illustrate religious stories. They prefer to design beautiful, intertwining patterns for embroidery and carpet weaving (so that we have the famous carpets of Persia) and to illustrate romantic poems and stories.

Let us look at one page of a book painted by a Persian artist at the end of the fourteenth century. The picture stands alongside the poem itself, which makes it just like an illustration in a modern book of fairy stories, except that in this case the work was all done by hand like the illuminated manuscripts of medieval times. The poem, which was written in the famous city of Baghdad, where Scheherazade told her thousand and one Tales of the Arabian Nights, is the story of the true love of a Persian prince for the daughter of a cruel Chinese emperor. He meets her while staying at the Chinese court, falls in love with her the minute he sees her, and goes through many exciting adventures and terrible misfortunes for her sake. One such misfortune is represented in this picture. The prince and princess meet by chance in the forest. Both are in armor, and as neither recognizes the other, they engage in a combat. The prince wounds the other knight, and the moment he does so, her helmet falls off, and he sees, to his great grief, that it is the woman he loves. Fortunately he has not harmed her too severely, and

149

Prince Humay Wounds Princess Humayun in Combat,
Persian Miniature, 14th Century

in the end, after many other adventures, they marry and live happily ever after.

As you can see, the forest is like a beautiful garden, all carpeted with flowers. The prince and princess are prepared for the combat according to tournament rules: each has come along on a horse all decked out with trappings and finery, like the horses on which the Crusaders rode to war. Tethering these fiery animals beside the flags stuck on top of tall poles to mark out the tournament ground, they have dismounted to engage with one another. Both of them wear armor all over, which explains why they were not able to recognize each other, and although the figures are rather small, you can just see that the prince's lance has pierced the princess's armor and her helmet is coming off. This picture, and the others like it in the same book, were painted for a tyrannical Persian ruler by one of the artists that he kept as favorites at his luxurious court. The artist was not very skillful at representing space, but he has made wonderful patterns out of the trees and flowers, and the sky is full of birds, as if the world in which his story-book characters moved was one of happiness and light. For many years before the fourteenth century, the Persians did not really have an art of their own. Then suddenly they combined Chinese ways of painting with the style that had been shared by all the Moslem world up to that time, and began to produce books like this one. The style was liked, and an artist of the next century illustrating the same sort of story would paint it in a way that is not very different from the way you see it painted here, putting in a high horizon line, making the ground tilt up steeply behind the flat little figures, and writing in one corner an expla-nation of what is happening in the picture. And so the painting of Persia became stylized, and like the painting of ancient Egypt or Europe during the Dark Ages, it did not change from generation to generation. These illustrations, because they are generally quite small, are called "miniatures."

Look next at a page of an Indian book called the *Khamsah*, painted in the seventeenth century. You will remember that Alexander the Great marched into India in the fourth century B.C. The

Alexander Breaks the Arm of the Ruler of the Kipchaks of China, Indian Miniature, 17th Century

Indians were much impressed by him, and after his death he turned into a great figure of legend about whom many stories were told, and were still being told two thousand years later when this picture was painted. Here we see Alexander in battle, breaking the arm of the ruler of the Kip-chaks of China. In the front of the picture are the horses of the two warriors, both stiff and flat, and the anatomy of the figures themselves is not correct. Alexander, who looks and is dressed more like an Oriental than a Greek, is in an impossible position, seemingly right on top of the Chinese ruler whose arm he is breaking. In the background there rise two flat mountains, with oversized men

From the British Museum, reproduced in Chinese Painting, by courtesy of Faber and Faber, Ltd.

Birds and Lichees, Chinese Painting, Ming Dynasty (1368–1644)

peering from behind them. Indeed this picture is stylized, like the work of the ancient Egyptians, and that of the Persians which it so much resembles, but how decorative it is, and how clearly it tells the story!

Now look at the Chinese painting of a bird sitting in the branches of an Eastern fruit tree. This tree bears a special fruit called the *lichee,* with a rough pinky-brown skin. What you see here is actually just one small section of a long scroll. When a Chinese is asked to show his treasures to a visitor, he will like to arrange his display around one very special work of art, rather than show a lot of things all at once, or one after the other, and he will give his visitor a long time in which to look at this treasure, and to study it and think about it. If he were going to show a scroll like the one of which we are speaking, he would perhaps arrange the room beforehand, hanging up a piece of lovely material on the wall, putting a piece of pottery or jade near by, and arranging a few flowers in a vase, all to provide a fitting background for what he wants to show. You would come in and sit down, and quietly look at the material and the vase, and this would put you in the right mood. Then your host would come forward and start showing you the scroll, unrolling it slowly, bit by bit. Do you see why? The scroll is too rich and complicated a treasure for you to take in all of it at once. And then it is painted with the same kind of picture all the way through. You are meant to study each bit of it in turn, with all the attention that you can manage. In this case you would notice how fond of nature the artist is: the Chinese think of man as by no means the most important thing in the universe, and believe that we should often lose ourselves in thought about the beauties of nature that surround us. You would also notice how perfectly shaped and colored each separate pink fruit is, and how soft-looking the birds' feathers are, and this might make you think about how marvelous the shape of fruit and the plumage of birds always appear, when you come to look at them with real attention, which is just what the Chinese artist, and also your Chinese host, intend you to do. Instead of

your having a lot of complicated things to see at once—as you would have if you studied nature by sitting outside in your orchard at home—the scroll offers you a few simple but perfect things on which to spend a great deal of time. After this experience, you will probably discover that you have learned to look at real birds and trees in new and exciting ways.

Chinese art, like the art of ancient Egypt, is dated according to the "dynasty," or ruling family, in whose time it was created.

The last Oriental work we have is a Japanese picture that is only about a century old, although it does not, perhaps, look that modern compared with some European pictures of the last hundred years. Actually this is a print, which means that the artist, instead of painting or drawing directly on canvas or paper, has cut lines deep into a block of wood or metal, covered this with paint or ink, and then clamped pieces of fine paper onto it, so that when the paper was pulled off again it carried the picture that he had designed. As we saw when we looked at the works of Dürer and Rembrandt, artists have known about this method, which makes it possible to produce a great many copies of the same picture, for many centuries, but it is only fairly recently that they have developed a technique for making a print in several colors. The print we are looking at shows boats entering Tempozan harbor in Japan. With the picture there comes a description that tells us that this harbor was a well-known place of great beauty at the time (it still is one today), and that it had a lovely name, being named after the "Mountain of the Heavenly Peace" that you see in the background. Prints like this were very popular with the Japanese because (besides being not too expensive) they provided a pleasant way of remembering what famous views of the country were like. If someone went traveling through Japan, and on the way made special journeys to look at beautiful mountains or waterfalls or ricefields or bridges, it was pleasing for him to be able to keep a record of what he had seen afterwards at home, just as many of us today take color photographs on our travels in order to have a way of remembering

From the Victoria and Albert Museum, reproduced in Japanese Landscape Prints, by courtesy of Faber and Faber, Ltd.

Ships Entering Tempozan Harbor, Japanese Print, 19th Century

how beautiful a lake that we visited one evening looked at sunset, and in order to be able to enjoy the pleasure over again. Yet this print, if you study it, is not really at all like a photograph. The sun's rays, for example, are colored pink because the artist had only a few colors to work with, and this one went well with the blues and blacks he used in other parts of the print. The ships are sailing in perfect arrowhead formation, making up a marvelous pattern, and the birds are probably put in overhead because the artist knew that a few such birds were always to be seen over the harbor, and so were a very familiar part of the view (just as we always think of an Atlantic liner with a few sea gulls flying over it). Now look at how the water is represented. For Japanese and Chinese artists the very act of using a brush or pen to make a particular stroke or line has a special importance. The way in which you make your strokes needs to match in special ways your feeling about what the thing that you are painting is like. Now, if you have sat watching the waves of the sea as they come in and break upon the shore, you will know that it is possible to get completely lost in following all the curves and changing patterns of the water. So in this case the artist has put together a pattern of lines and curves which we easily recognize as standing for the crests of the waves, though of course he has not painted water at all. Perhaps you can work out for yourself in the same kind of way what the artist feels the ships and sun and mountain to be really like.

The art of primitive peoples in Africa and throughout the world might really have a chapter to itself, for it is quite different again from Oriental art. We talk of it sometimes as "primitive art," because it is produced by peoples who are still only at a very early or primitive stage of development and live the way the peoples of Europe and Asia lived many thousands of years ago, before the beginning of history. These peoples may live in the jungles, or in hill country, or in the least explored parts of Africa, America, or the South Seas. Their life is very simple. They have strange rituals and dances; they kill wild animals for food with simple spears and arrows; and they have long

fables and native stories that they recite to one another around the open fire. They live in huts or simple camps built of wood or stone, and wear rough clothes made of bark or animal hide. One very important part of their lives is the carving of objects in wood and stone, and many of the things they use in everyday life, such as headdresses or canoes or fishhooks, are artistically made. It is only quite recently that we have studied objects of this kind and learned to look on them as beautiful in themselves. Because we now find them beautiful, we refer to them as "art." But it is important to remember that for the people who made them they are not objects to be looked at, or to be kept in collections, but objects to be used from day to day in the routine of their lives.

Why do primitive peoples devote so much time and trouble to work of this sort? Let us look at some of the ways in which they use what they make.

First, there are religious objects—statues and totem poles and little figures meant to stand beside the family hearth. Like the earliest peoples of Europe, these people worship very simple gods, such as a god of rain or a god of the harvest, or the ghost of an ancestor. If the tribesmen are afraid of a god who can send down thunder or lightning, or of a god who watches over the dead, they will carve shapes that express what a frightening character he has. For festivals and solemn occasions, they will put offerings of food and drink before the statues, and will perform special rituals in which their statues and totem poles are carried around from place to place. It all means a tremendous amount in their lives, and so a great deal of care and skill goes into the making of the figures and emblems. Look at the beautifully carved statue of a couple, probably representing ancestors of the family to which they belong in West Africa. The figures are stylized, like those we saw in ancient Egypt, with circular slits for eyes and straight slits for mouths, and they certainly are not portraits of the particular people they represent, but like the works of modern art we have seen, they present a pleasing pattern, and we can enjoy the beauty of the hard, shiny wood from which they

Seated Couple,
from the Ivory Coast

were so carefully and skillfully carved.

Secondly, there are objects used for fancy dress on special occasions, such as the festivals and celebrations that play a very important part in everyone's life. Each tribe may have its own colors and plumage and kinds of dress. When the time comes, the tribesmen will bring out the masks and headdresses and beads and drums and rattles that they have been preparing for many months, and everyone will contribute something to the occasion. Let us look at the "Firespitter" mask from the Ivory Coast in Africa. It is meant to represent the head of a deerlike animal, and when it is used in a dance, smoke comes out of its mouth, although we do not know how the natives manage to do this. Notice what a pleasing pattern the design of the face makes, and what a lovely line is formed by the antlers. If the mask is terrifying, it is also beautiful in a way.

"Firespitter" Mask, from the Ivory Coast

157

Lastly, there are objects of everyday use, such as tables and chairs and cups and shoes and buttons and earrings and hunting knives. Many tribes or peoples have long traditions of craftsmanship. They pass down from father to son and mother to daughter the way in which to bake a simple clay plate or to carve the front of a canoe or to weave a covering for a bed. See, for example, the very decorative way some craftsman of Tahiti has fashioned a fly whisk, or how carefully patterns have been cut into the flat side of a throwing knife from the Congo. These knives are oddly shaped so that they can be thrown at the feet of an enemy and trip him up. Nobody has any desire to be very original, but only to produce something just like what his neighbor is using, and just as good and practical for the purpose that it is intended to serve.

You can learn a lot from the best examples of primitive art—about how a bit of braid and a pebble can stand for the whole face of a god, and how a few deep-cut lines can show a god's anger and power, and how a mask with curved slits cut in it for the eyes can be a very beautiful object.

Now you have seen how men everywhere, and from very earliest times, have tried to portray the world they see around them and the emotions they feel within, and that this is called "art." Wherever we have found art, it has been the mirror of the age and people that produced it, reflecting their dress and manner and what they found to be important. Above all, in creating art, men have always tried to make something they felt to be beautiful; and when we too find beauty in what they have created, we come close to understanding them, whatever the country or century in which they live.

Courtesy of the Museum of Primitive Art, and photographed by Charles Uht

Fly Whisk, from Tahiti

Throwing Knife, from the Congo
Courtesy of the Museum of Primitive Art, and photographed by Charles Uht